John Milton

L'Allegro
and
Il Penseroso

Edited by
Elaine B. Safer
Thomas L. Erskine
University of Delaware

The Merrill Literary
Casebook Series
Edward P. J. Corbett, Editor

Charles E. Merrill Publishing Company
A Bell & Howell Company
Columbus, Ohio

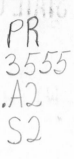
Standard Book Number: 675-09361-9

Library of Congress Catalog Number: 77-108610

1 2 3 4 5 6 7 8 9 10 — 73 72 71 70

Printed in the United States of America

Foreword

The Charles E. Merrill Literary Casebook Series deals with short literary works, arbitrarily defined here as "works which can be easily read in a single sitting." Accordingly, the series will concentrate on poems, short stories, brief dramas, and literary essays. These casebooks are designed to be used in literature courses or in practical criticism courses where the instructor wants to expose his students to an extensive and intensive study of a single, short work or in composition courses where the instructor wants to expose his students to the discipline of writing a research paper on a literary text.

All of the casebooks in the series follow this format: (1) foreword; (2) general instructions for the writing of a research paper; (3) the editor's Introduction; (4) the text of the literary work; (5) a number of critical articles on the literary work; (6) suggested topics for short papers on the literary work; (7) suggested topics for long (10-15 pages) papers on the literary work; (8) a selective bibliography of additional readings on the literary work. Some of the casebooks, especially those dealing with poetry, may carry an additional section, which contains such features as variant versions of the work, a closely related literary work, comments by the author and his contemporaries on the work.

So that students might simulate first-hand research in library copies of books and bound periodicals, each of the critical articles carries full bibliographical information at the bottom of the first page of the article, and the text of the article carries the actual page-numbers of the original source. A notation like /131/ after a word in the text indicates that *after* that word in the original source the article went over to page 131. All of the text between that number and the next number, /132/, can be taken as occurring on page 131 of the original source.

Edward P.J. Corbett
General Editor

Contents

Introduction

Life and Background

John Milton was born in London on December 9, 1608, nine years after Edmund Spenser died. At this time William Shakespeare was forty-four; John Donne and Ben Jonson were thirty-six. Milton can be considered the last of the poets in the Elizabethan tradition, which is typified by the melodious sweetness and rich imagery of Spenser and Shakespeare. His companion poems, "L'Allegro" and "Il Penseroso," are reminiscent of Spenser's *Epithalamion* and many passages from Shakespeare's plays (e.g., *A Midsummer Night's Dream* and *Much Ado About Nothing*). The twin poems reveal little, if any, of the metaphysical wit of John Donne, but they do show indebtedness to the classical style of Ben Jonson's lyrics.

"L'Allegro" and "Il Penseroso" were published in Milton's first volume of poems in 1645, but their date of composition is uncertain. They may have been written during a vacation in Milton's last years at Cambridge, where he received his M.A. in 1631, or possibly during the following years when he lived with his parents on their country estate at Horton. They may be an outgrowth of his first academic prolusion—"Whether Day or Night is the more excellent"—and for this reason we have reprinted the prolusion, a seventeenth-century equivalent of a term paper.[1]

"L'Allegro" and "Il Penseroso" belong to what can be considered Milton's first period, the early poems (through 1640), which reflect the youthful Milton's delight in the sensuous and romantic works of the Latin poet Ovid, as well as the Puritan writer's increasing dedication

---

[1]See E.M.W. Tillyard's essay. Comparisons have also been made between the sixth and seventh prolusions and the poems.

1

to ethical and religious subjects. The poems also show Milton's early experimentation with traditional forms, such as the Latin elegy, the Italian sonnet, and the pastoral. These include the six Latin elegies, the first seven (of his twenty-three) sonnets, "Death of a Fair Infant Dying of a Cough," "At a Vacation Exercise," the "Nativity Ode, At a Solemn Music," the masque *Comus,* "Lycidas," and Milton's elegy to his closest friend Charles Diodati, "Epitaphium Damonis."

"L'Allegro" and "Il Penseroso" are a pastoral celebration of an ideal day. The lilting movement of their octosyllabic couplets evokes a peaceful quality suggesting a vacation from the workaday world. Their tone differs from that of the amatory verse—e.g., "Elegy V," "Elegy VII" and the Italian sonnets—and also from the austere quality present in many of Milton's early works. The poems lack the solemn stress on the disciplined life of the poet in "Elegy VI," who "ought himself to be a true poem" (*Apology for Smectymnuus,* 1642), the social concern of the passage on the corrupt clergy in "Lycidas," and the strong ethical emphasis of the "Nativity Ode," where Christ's routing of the pagan demons exemplifies truth overcoming error.

The idyllic poems were written by the young Milton before he became engaged in pamphlet warfare (1641-1660) over the religious and political controversies in seventeenth-century England. They were written before Milton's unhappy marriage to Mary Powell (1642) and before Milton became blind (1652) and felt the need to justify his blindness as a gift of divine illumination rather than a punishment from God, as many of his vitriolic critics claimed. "L'Allegro" and "Il Penseroso" lack the sober social criticism evidenced in Milton's final plea for the Commonwealth (*The Ready and Easy Way to Establish a Free Commonwealth,* 1660) where he sorrowfully spoke out against the "misguided and abused multitude" for willfully giving up all the freedom it had fought for.

The companion poems also lack the underlying pessimism exhibited in the poetry of Milton's last period: the great epic, *Paradise Lost,* the brief epic, *Paradise Regained,* and the tragedy, *Samson Agonistes.* In all these works, beneath the belief in man's future redemption is the awareness of the pain and woe of this world "Under her own weight groaning," the picture of man who has lost Paradise and who is inclined to re-enact the Fall of Adam and Eve. The lively, sociable tone of "L'Allegro" and "Il Penseroso" reveals a peace of mind, a luxuriating in the ideal, which is quite different. Their apparent simplicity and light tone are similar to that of Milton's early lyric, "Song: on May Morning" (ca., 1631).

The Poems — A Brief Introduction and Survey of Criticism

Milton followed definite literary conventions in writing "L'Allegro and "Il Penseroso": the pastoral (which delicately depicts the simplicity and beauty of rustic life—shepherds tending their flock, piping on reeds, appreciating the joys of nature) ; the academic debate (e.g., the *First Prolusion*) ; companion poems (witty Renaissance debates like Christopher Marlowe's "The Passionate Shepherd to his Love" and Sir Walter Ralegh's cynical answer, "The Nymph's Reply to the Shepherd"; John Fletcher's "Hence, All You Vain Delights" and William Strode's reply, "Return My Joys") ; and prose character sketches (e.g., Joseph Hall's *Characters of Virtues and Vices,* which has sketches of the Happy Man, the Humble Man, and the Wise Man).[2]

"L'Allegro" and "Il Penseroso" are written in octosyllabic couplets of varying iambic and trochaic rhythms, except for their prologues of trimeter and tetrameter lines. At the opening of each, the subject of the other is distorted and rejected. These stereotyped and exaggerated positions are later shown to be absurd through the depiction of the simple joys of the speaker of each poem. The genealogy of the Goddess of Mirth and of Melancholy is given next, and the companions of each are personified. The chief companion of Mirth is "the mountain-nymph, sweet Liberty." Others are described:

> Jest and youthful jollity,
> Quips and cranks and wanton wiles,
> Nods, and becks and wreathed smiles . . .
> Sport that wrinkled Care derides,
> And Laughter holding both his sides.

The chief companion of Melancholy is "The Cherub Contemplation." Others, including Silence, are described:

> calm Peace and Quiet,
> Spare Fast, that oft with gods doth diet . . .
> And add to these retired Leisure,
> That in trim gardens takes his pleasure.

These personifications are magnificently developed through a lilting movement in "L'Allegro" and a more dignified, subdued pace in "Il Penseroso," where religious imagery (*pensive Nun, rapt soul, Spare*

---

[2] See articles by J. B. Leishman and Maren-Sofie Røstvig.

Fast, Jove's altar) prepare us for the soft music of the nightingale, rather than for the loud, cheerful sounds of a dawn scene (the lark and the cock; the hounds and horn).

Critics have questioned whether to read the companion poems as balanced complements or contrasts—between day and night, mirth and melancholy, fancy and reality, activity and contemplation, gregariousness and solitude, the Cavalier and the Puritan way of life— or as a unified progression, culminating in the mystical experience of the Pensive Man. Twentieth-century interpretation of the poems ranges from dismissing them as "ponderous trifles"[3] to acclaiming them for their simplicity (E. M. W. Tillyard), for their universality for every man (Rosemond Tuve), and for their serious development of the 'Prophetic strain' (Don Cameron Allen).

The essays in this book start with an excerpt from Samuel Johnson's *The Lives of the Poets* and continue with the biographical approach of Thomas Warton, who uses Milton's personality as a means of unifying aspects of the poems. For him there is a subdued quality in both poems, which reflects the serious bent of Milton himself. Warton points to the landscape in "L'Allegro" that "wears a shade of pensiveness" on its "*russet* lawns, *fallows gray*, and *barren* mountains, overhung with *labouring* clouds." For Warton: "Even his [Milton's] most brilliant imagery is mellowed with the sober hues of philosophic meditation."

The articles by Lawrence Babb and J. B. Leishman help establish the seventeenth-century background for the companion poems: the two conceptions of melancholy held in the Renaissance, and the similarities between Milton's poems and others of his day. Such historical appraisal is as important for the twentieth-century reader as an understanding of modern technology and Freudian psychology would be for the Renaissance man, if he were to appreciate modern literature.

A collection of studies such as this also enables us to see how critics respond to each other's commentaries. For example, T. S. Eliot, in his 1936 essay, criticized Milton's lack of visual imagination ("The imagery in *L'Allegro* and *Il Penseroso* is all general") and complained that his images lacked vibrancy ("Milton writes English like a dead language"). Eliot's comments ushered in a new phase of Milton criticism: the complaint that a "dissociation of sensibility,"[4] a separa-

[3]William Empson, "Thy Darling in an Urn," *Sewanee Review*, LV (1947), 691.
[4]See "The Metaphysical Poets," in *Selected Essays 1917-1932* (New York: Harcourt, Brace & World, 1960).

tion of thought and feeling, exists in the poetry of John Milton. We can glimpse the reaction to Eliot by Phyllis MacKenzie's explication of imagery, by J. B. Leishman's comments on the effectiveness of "evocation rather than scene painting," and by the interpretation of different aspects of Milton's imagery (before rarely the subject of criticism), by Cleanth Brooks, Kester Svendsen, Don Cameron Allen, Rosemond Tuve, and J. Milton French.

Cleanth Brooks closely examines the day-night contrast in the poems and concludes that the "cool half-lights" (of neither "flaring sunbeam" nor "unreleaved blackness") are "a sort of symbol of the aesthetic distance which the cheerful man, no less than the pensive man, consistently maintains." He, like many modern critics, shows how imagery is used to create paradox: in the twin poems, there is "tension between the two choices . . . which can appeal to the same mind." Responding to Brooks are Kester Svendsen (who expands the discussion of imagery to include sound and music) and J. Milton French (who examines the light imagery in an effort to disprove Brooks's basic tenets).

This collection of studies attempts to point to how "L'Allegro" and "Il Penseroso" influenced later poetry. Maren-Sofie Røstvig examines their effect on the "Happy Man" motif in eighteenth-century poetry. In the suggested readings, we mention Raymond Dexter Havens,[5] who traces the influence of Milton's companion poems on the poetry of the mid-eighteenth century, particularly on the works of such prominent poets as William Collins (e.g., the odes "Pity" and "The Passions"), Thomas Gray (e.g., "Hymn to Adversity" and "Ode for Music"), and Thomas Warton (e.g., the blank-verse "Pleasures of Melancholy" and "Ode on the Approach of Summer").

In the eighteenth century, to imitate the companion poems became so great a fad that they and their admirers were the subject of popular parodies, such as George Colman and Robert Lloyd's odes "To Obscurity" and "To Oblivion" (1759), which mocked the poems of Gray and William Mason, and the anonymous "Garrulous Man, a Parody upon L'Allegro of Milton" (1777). Havens has pointed out that from 1760 to 1800, two hundred and seventy-five pieces were influenced by "L'Allegro" and "Il Penseroso."[6] The popularity of the companion poems waned at the close of the eighteenth century, but we are still able to see traces of them in the romantic poets, particu-

---

[5]*The Influence of Milton on English Poetry* (New York: Russell & Russell, 1961; orig. pub. 1922).
[6]*Ibid.*, p. 469.

larly in Samuel Taylor Coleridge ("To Disappointment," 1792) and Percy Bysshe Shelley ("To Jane: the Invitation," 1824).

In the twentieth century, the poems are often considered Milton's most popular. Because they are brief and contain many of the devices and themes developed in Milton's later works, "L'Allegro" and "Il Penseroso" are frequently taught in undergraduate courses. The primary aim of this collection of essays is to make available some of the best comments on the twin poems in order to show the numerous possibilities of interpretation that they offer. We thus hope to stimulate rereading and reconsideration of the poems so that students will more fully appreciate their subtleties, their paradoxes, their beauty. We hope to get "L'Allegro" and "Il Penseroso" "out of Closets and libraries, Schools and Colleges, to dwell in Clubs and Assemblies, at Tea-Tables and Coffee-Houses."

L'Allegro*

Hence, loathèd Melancholy,
    Of Cerberus and blackest Midnight born
In Stygian cave forlorn,
    'Mongst horrid shapes, and shrieks, and sights unholy!
Find out some uncouth cell,   5
    Where brooding Darkness spreads his jealous wings,
And the night-raven sings;
    There under ebon shades and low-browed rocks,
As ragged as thy locks,
    In dark Cimmerian desert ever dwell.   10
But come, thou goddess fair and free,
In Heaven yclept Euphrosyne,
And by men heart-easing Mirth;
Whom lovely Venus, at a birth,
With two sister Graces more,   15
To ivy-crownèd Bacchus bore:
Or whether (as some sager sing)
The frolic wind that breathes the spring,
Zephyr, with Aurora playing,
As he met her once a-Maying,   20
There on beds of violets blue,
And fresh-blown roses washed in dew,

---

*The modernized text of Milton's two poems is reprinted from Julian W. Aber-
nethy's edition, *Lycidas, Comus, L'Allegro, Il Penseroso and Other Poems* (New
York: Charles E. Merrill, 1906). 1 *Cerberus:* the three-headed dog that guards the
gates of Hell. Milton invents this account of Melancholy's genealogy. 3 *Stygian:*
pertaining to the Styx, one of the four rivers of Hell; dark or gloomy as the region
of the Styx. 5 *uncouth:* strange, unknown. 8 *ebon:* black. 10 *Cimmerian:* in
Homer's *Odyssey* the land of the Cimmerians is described as one of perpetual darkness. 11 *fair and free:* traditional poetic epithets denoting beauty and grace.
12 *yclept:* named. *Euphrosyne: Mirth*, one of the Graces. Her two sisters were
Aglaia (Brightness) and Thalia (Bloom). 14-16 *Venus:* one traditionally accepted
parentage of the Graces was Venus (goddess of love) and Bacchus (god of wine).
Milton invents the other genealogy. 18 *frolic:* frolicsome, sportive. 19 *Zephyr:*
the west wind. *Aurora:* the dawn.

Filled her with thee, a daughter fair,
So buxom, blithe, and debonair.
Haste thee, nymph, and bring with thee   25
Jest and youthful jollity,
Quips and cranks and wanton wiles,
Nods and becks and wreathèd smiles,
Such as hang on Hebe's cheek,
And love to live in dimple sleek;   30
Sport that wrinkled Care derides,
And Laughter holding both his sides.
Come, and trip it as you go,
On the light fantastic toe;
And in thy right hand lead with thee   35
The mountain-nymph, sweet Liberty;
And if I give thee honor due,
Mirth, admit me of thy crew,
To live with her, and live with thee
In unreprovèd pleasures free;   40
To hear the lark begin his flight,
And, singing, startle the dull night,
From his watch-tower in the skies,
Till the dappled dawn doth rise;
Then to come, in spite of sorrow,   45
And at my window bid good morrow,
Through the sweetbrier or the vine,
Or the twisted eglantine;
While the cock, with lively din,
Scatters the rear of darkness thin,   50
And to the stack, or the barn door,
Stoutly struts his dames before:
Oft listening how the hounds and horn
Cheerly rouse the slumbering morn,
From the side of some hoar hill,   55
Through the high wood echoing shrill:
Sometime walking, not unseen,
By hedgerow elms, on hillocks green,
Right against the eastern gate

---

24 *buxom:* obliging, gay. *debonair:* gracious, of gentle disposition. 27 *cranks:*
fanciful turns of speech. 28 *becks:* beckoning gestures, perhaps bows and curtseys.
29 *Hebe's:* pertaining to the goddess of youth. 33 *trip it:* dance. 38 *crew:*
company. 40 *unreprovèd:* innocent. 55 *hoar:* as Hubert H. Hoeltje points out
(see Additional Readings), the term is "descriptive of the mist-covered hills of any

Where the great sun begins his state,   60
Robed in flames and amber light,
The clouds in thousand liveries dight;
While the plowman, near at hand,
Whistles o'er the furrowed land,
And the milkmaid singeth blithe,   65
And the mower whets his scythe,
And every shepherd tells his tale
Under the hawthorn in the dale.
Straight mine eye hath caught new pleasures,
Whilst the landskip round it measures: 70
Russet lawns and fallows gray,
Where the nibbling flocks do stray;
Mountains on whose barren breast
The laboring clouds do often rest;
Meadows trim with daisies pied,   75
Shallow brooks and rivers wide;
Towers and battlements it sees
Bosomed high in tufted trees,
Where perhaps some beauty lies,
The Cynosure of neighboring eyes.   80
Hard by, a cottage chimney smokes
From betwixt two aged oaks,
Where Corydon and Thyrsis met
Are at their savory dinner set
Of herbs and other country messes,   85
Which the neat-handed Phillis dresses;
And then in haste her bower she leaves,
With Thestylis to bind the sheaves;
Or, if the earlier season lead,
To the tanned haycock in the mead.   90
Sometimes with secure delight
The upland hamlets will invite,
When the merry bells ring round,
And the jocund rebecks sound

---

dewy summer morning, when an observer ... will notice that the slopes seem literally white." 60 *state:* stately progress. 62 *liveries:* gorgeous costumes (Hughes). *dight:* arrayed, dressed. 67 *tells his tale:* counts his sheep. 70 *landskip:* landscape. 75 *pied:* marked with different shades or colors. 78 *bosomed:* enclosed. 83 *Corydon and Thrysis:* with Phillis and Thestylis, names of rustics associated with the pastoral tradition. 85 *messes:* prepared dishes. 87 *bower:* rustic dwelling, cottage. 91 *secure:* carefree. 94 *rebecks:* an early form of the fiddle.

To many a youth and many a maid,   95
Dancing in the chequered shade;
And young and old come forth to play
On a sunshine holiday,
Till the livelong daylight fail:
Then to the spicy nut-brown ale,   100
With stories told of many a feat,
How Faery Mab the junkets eat:
She was pinched and pulled, she said;
And he, by Friar's lantern led,
Tells how the drudging goblin sweat   105
To earn his cream-bowl duly set,
When in one night, ere glimpse of morn,
His shadowy flail hath threshed the corn
That ten day-laborers could not end;
Then lies him down, the lubber fiend,   110
And, stretched out all the chimney's length,
Basks at the fire his hairy strength;
And crop-full out of doors he flings,
Ere the first cock his matin rings.
Thus done the tales, to bed they creep,   115
By whispering winds soon lulled asleep
Towered cities please us then,
And the busy hum of men,
Where throngs of knights and barons bold,
In weeds of peace, high triumphs hold,   120
With store of ladies, whose bright eyes
Rain influence, and judge the prize
Of wit or arms, while both contend
To win her grace whom all commend.
There let Hymen oft appear   125
In saffron robe, with taper clear,
And pomp, and feast, and revelry,
With mask, and antique pageantry;
Such sights as youthful poets dream

---

102 *Faery Mab:* queen of the fairies. 103 *she:* with *he* (104), the tellers of the tales. 104 *Friar's lantern:* the will-o'-the-wisp. 105 The terms *goblin* and *lubber fiend* (110) probably refer to the legendary Robin Goodfellow, who was noted for his mischievous deeds and for the tremendous amount of work he could do when motivated by food. 113 *crop-full:* with stomach filled. 120 *weeds:* garments. *triumphs:* festivals of victory. 121 *store of:* many. 122 *influence:* the ladies' eyes, like the stars, act upon the destiny of men. 125 *Hymen:* god of marriage.

On summer eves by haunted stream.   130
Then to the well-trod stage anon,
If Jonson's learnèd sock be on,
Or sweetest Shakspere, Fancy's child,
Warble his native wood-notes wild.
And ever, against eating cares,   135
Lap me in soft Lydian airs,
Married to immortal verse,
Such as the meeting soul may pierce,
In notes with many a winding bout
Of linkèd sweetness long drawn out   140
With wanton heed and giddy cunning,
The melting voice through mazes running,
Untwisting all the chains that tie
The hidden soul of harmony;
That Orpheus' self may heave his head   145
From golden slumber on a bed
Of heaped Elysian flowers, and hear
Such strains as would have won the ear
Of Pluto to have quite set free
His half-regained Eurydice.   150
These delights if thou canst give,
Mirth, with thee I mean to live.

---

132 *sock:* the light shoe worn by actors in Greek and Roman comedy; it is thus an allusion to Ben Jonson's comedies. 136 *Lydian:* soft, sweet music, as opposed to the music in the Dorian and Phrygian modes. 139 *bout:* a round; "here a stretch or movement of music" (Prince). 145 *Orpheus:* in Greek mythology the famous singer and musician who "half-regained" his wife Eurydice from Hades (the underworld) by charming Proserpina and Pluto with his music. He lost her because he could not comply with Pluto's condition that he not look back at her until they were completely out of the underworld. 147 *Elysian:* pertaining to Elysium, the Greek paradise for the dead.

Il Penseroso

Hence, vain deluding Joys,
   The brood of Folly without father bred!
How little you bestead,
   Or fill the fixèd mind with all your toys!
Dwell in some idle brain,   5
   And fancies fond with gaudy shapes possess,
As thick and numberless
   As the gay motes that people the sunbeams,
Or likest hovering dreams,
   The fickle pensioners of Morpheus' train.   10
But hail, thou goddess, sage and holy,
Hail, divinest Melancholy!
Whose saintly visage is too bright
To hit the sense of human sight,
And therefore to our weaker view   15
O'erlaid with black, staid Wisdom's hue;
Black, but such as in esteem
Prince Memnon's sister might beseem,
Or that starred Ethiop queen that strove
To set her beauty's praise above   20
The sea-nymphs', and their powers offended.
Yet thou art higher far descended:
Thee bright-hair'd Vesta long of yore
To solitary Saturn bore;

---

3 *bestead:* help, assist. 4 *toys:* trifles. 6 *fond:* foolish. 10 *pensioners:* attendants. *Morpheus:* god of sleep. 14 *hit:* agree with. 18 *Prince Memnon's sister:* in his *Odyssey,* Homer praises the beauty and prowess of the Ethiopean Prince Memnon, and Milton assumes that his sister, Hemera, was also beautiful. *beseem:* become, suit. 19 *Ethiop queen:* Cassiopeia, who was turned into a constellation *(starred)* for boasting that her daughter Andromeda's beauty was greater than that of the "sea-nymphs" (the Nereids). 23 *Vesta:* Virgin goddess of the domestic hearth. Milton invents Melancholy's genealogy. 24 *Saturn:* ruler of the gods during the Golden Age. In astrology, people born under the sign of the planet Saturn

His daughter she; in Saturn's reign,   25
Such mixture was not held a stain.
Oft in glimmering bowers and glades
He met her, and in secret shades
Of woody Ida's inmost grove,
Whilst yet there was no fear of Jove.   30
Come, pensive Nun, devout and pure,
Sober, steadfast, and demure,
All in a robe of darkest grain,
Flowing with majestic train,
And sable stole of cypress lawn,   35
Over thy decent shoulders drawn.
Come, but keep thy wonted state,
With even step, and musing gait,
And looks commércing with the skies,
Thy rapt soul sitting in thine eyes: 40
There, held in holy passion still,
Forget thyself to marble, till
With a sad leaden downward cast
Thou fix them on the earth as fast.
And join with thee calm Peace, and Quiet,   45
Spare Fast, that oft with gods doth diet,
And hears the Muses in a ring
Aye round about Jove's altar sing;
And add to these retired Leisure,
That in trim gardens takes his pleasure;   50
But, first and chiefest, with thee bring
Him that yon soars on golden wing,
Guiding the fiery-wheeled throne,
The Cherub Contemplation;
And the mute Silence hist along,   55

---

are supposed to be serious and melancholic. 29 *Ida's inmost grove:* Mount Ida, in Greece, where Saturn reigned. 30 *Jove:* Saturn's son, who rebelled and usurped his father's throne. 33 *grain:* color. 35 *cypress lawn:* a fine, black material. 36 *decent:* modest. 37 *wonted state:* customary stately progress. 39 *commércing:* communicating with. 42 *forget thyself to marble:* become so lost in contemplation that you resemble a statue. 43 *sad:* serious. *leaden:* lead was associated with Saturn. Masson says that Melancholy's "eyes had the leaden hue of the blast from her father's star." 44 *as fast:* as firmly (as you fixed them on Heaven). 46 *diet:* dine. 48 *Aye:* ever. 53 *fiery-wheeled throne:* see the description of the throne of God in Ezekiel, X. 54 *Cherub Contemplation:* the Cherubim, the second order of angels, were thought to be capable of contemplating and knowing divine things. 55 *hist:* summon.

'Less Philomel will deign a song,
In her sweetest, saddest plight,
Smoothing the rugged brow of Night,
While Cynthia checks her dragon yoke
Gently o'er the accustomed oak.   60
Sweet bird, that shunn'st the noise of folly,
Most musical, most melancholy!
Thee, chauntress, oft the woods among
I woo, to hear thy even-song;
And, missing thee, I walk unseen   65
On the dry smooth-shaven green,
To behold the wandering moon,
Riding near her highest noon,
Like one that had been led astray
Through the heaven's wide pathless way,   70
And oft, as if her head she bowed,
Stooping through a fleecy cloud.
Oft, on a plat of rising ground,
I hear the far-off curfew sound,
Over some wide-watered shore,   75
Swinging slow with sullen roar;
Or, if the air will not permit,
Some still removèd place will fit,
Where glowing embers through the room
Teach light to counterfeit a gloom,   80
Far from all resort of mirth,
Save the cricket on the hearth,
Or the bellman's drowsy charm
To bless the doors from nightly harm.
Or let my lamp at midnight hour   85
Be seen in some high lonely tower,
Where I may oft outwatch the Bear,
With thrice-great Hermes, or unsphere
The spirit of Plato, to unfold

---

56 *'Less:* unless. *Philomel:* the nightingale. *deign:* grant. 57 *plight:* mood.
59 *Cynthia:* goddess of the moon. *dragon yoke:* pair of yoked dragons which draw
the moon's chariot. 63 *chauntress:* female singer; possibly retains its Middle
English meaning, enchantress. 68 *highest noon:* the place of the moon at midnight.
73 *plat:* small plot of ground. 83 *bellman's drowsy charm:* the sing-song or cry
of the night watchman, who called the hours. 87 *outwatch the Bear:* since the
constellation of the Bear (Ursa Major) never sets, the meaning of this phrase is to
stay awake all night. 88-9 *thrice-great Hermes:* Hermes Trismegistus, the Egyptian
Thoth, who was thought to be the author of many mystical and philosophical books.

What worlds or what vast regions hold 90
The immortal mind, that hath forsook
Her mansion in this fleshly nook;
And of those demons that are found
In fire, air, flood, or under ground,
Whose power hath a true consent 95
With planet or with element.
Sometimes let gorgeous Tragedy
In sceptered pall come sweeping by,
Presenting Thebes, or Pelops' line,
Or the tale of Troy divine, 100
Or what (though rare) of later age
Ennobled hath the buskined stage.
But, O sad Virgin! that thy power
Might raise Musæus from his bower;
Or bid the soul of Orpheus sing 105
Such notes as, warbled to the string,
Drew iron tears down Pluto's cheek,
And made Hell grant what love did seek;
Or call up him that left half-told
The story of Cambuscan bold, 110
Of Camball and of Algarsife,
And who had Canace to wife,
That owned the virtuous ring and glass,
And of the wondrous horse of brass
On which the Tartar king did ride; 115
And if aught else great bards beside
In sage and solemn tunes have sung,
Of tourneys, and of trophies hung,
Of forests and enchantments drear,
Where more is meant than meets the ear. 120
Thus, Night, oft see me in thy pale career,

---

unsphere the spirit of Plato: draw the spirit of Plato down from the heavenly sphere where it dwells. 92 *fleshly nook:* body. 93 *demons:* spirits ruling the four elements in l. 94. 95 *consent:* concord. 98 *sceptered pall:* royal robe. 99-100 *Thebes, Pelops' line, Troy:* Oedipus, King of Thebes; Agamemnon, Orestes, Electra, Iphigenia — descendants of Pelops; and the Trojan War. These provided material for the Greek tragedians Aeschylus, Sophocles, and Euripides. 102 *buskined:* a reference to the high shoe worn by actors in Greek tragedy, commonly a symbol for tragedy. 104 *Musæus:* mythical Greek poet, sometimes referred to as the son of Orpheus. 105 *Orpheus:* see "L'Allegro," ll. 145-50 and note. 110 *Cambuscan:* with *Camball, Algarsife,* and *Canace,* characters in Chaucer's unfinished *Squire's Tale.* 113 *virtuous:* endowed with magical powers. 121 *career:* course.

Till civil-suited Morn appear,
Not tricked and frounced, as she was wont
With the Attic boy to hunt,
But kerchieft in a comely cloud,   125
While rocking winds are piping loud,
Or ushered with a shower still,
When the gust hath blown his fill,
Ending on the rustling leaves,
With minute-drops from off the eaves.   130
And, when the sun begins to fling
His flaring beams, me, Goddess, bring
To archèd walks of twilight groves,
And shadows brown, that Sylvan loves,
Of pine, or monumental oak,   135
Where the rude ax with heavèd stroke
Was never heard the nymphs to daunt,
Or fright them from their hallowed haunt.
There, in close covert, by some brook,
Where no profaner eye may look,   140
Hide me from day's garish eye,
While the bee with honeyed thigh,
That at her flowery work doth sing,
And the waters murmuring,
With such consort as they keep,   145
Entice the dewy-feathered Sleep;
And let some strange mysterious Dream
Wave at his wings, in airy stream
Of lively portraiture displayed,
Softly on my eyelids laid;   150
And, as I wake, sweet music breathe
Above, about, or underneath,
Sent by some Spirit to mortals good,
Or the unseen Genius of the wood.
But let my due feet never fail   155
To walk the studious cloister's pale,

---

122 *civil-suited:* plainly dressed. 123 *tricked:* adorned. *frounced:* with hair
curled. 124 *Attic boy:* Cephalus, loved by Aurora, goddess of the dawn. 130
minute-drops: drops falling every minute. 134 *brown:* dark. *Sylvan:* Sylvanus,
woodland god. 145 *consort:* companionship, harmony. 147-8 *And let some mysterious dream/Wave at his wings:* Masson suggests the following: "Let some mysterious dream wave (i.e., move to and fro) at his (i.e., Sleep's) wings." 154
Genius: presiding spirit. 156 *pale:* enclosure.

And love the high embowèd roof,
With antique pillars massy-proof,
And storied windows richly dight,
Casting a dim religious light.   160
There let the pealing organ blow,
To the full-voiced quire below,
In service high, and anthems clear,
As may with sweetness, through mine ear,
Dissolve me into ecstasies,   165
And bring all heaven before mine eyes.
And may at last my weary age
Find out the peaceful hermitage,
The hairy gown and mossy cell,
Where I may sit and rightly spell   170
Of every star that heaven doth shew,
And every herb that sips the dew,
Till old experience do attain
To something like prophetic strain.
These pleasures, Melancholy, give,   175
And I with thee will choose to live.

---

157 *embowèd*: arched. 158 *antique pillars*: extravagantly, perhaps fantastically, decorated columns. *massy-proof*: so massive as to be proof against the weight they support. 159 *storied windows*: stained-glass windows, depicting scenes from the Bible. *dight*: adorned. 169 *hairy gown*: probably the rough, coarse gown worn by monks and hermits, not the hair shirt worn by penitents (Abernethy). 170 *spell*: consider, contemplate.

John Milton

First Prolusion*

Some of the Author's Preliminary Academic Exercises

I   Delivered in College

Whether Day or Night is the more excellent

It is a frequent maxim of the most eminent masters of rhetoric, as you know well, Members of the University, that in every style of oration, whether demonstrative, deliberative, or judicial, the speaker must begin by winning the good-will of his audience; without it he cannot make any impression upon them, nor succeed as he would wish in his cause. If this be so (and, to tell the truth, I know that the learned are all agreed in regarding it as an established axiom), how unfortunate I am and to what a pass am I brought this day! At the very outset of my oration I fear I shall have to say something contrary to all the rules of oratory, and be forced to depart from the first and chief duty of an orator. For how can I hope for your good-will, when in all this great assembly I encounter none but hostile glances, so that my task seems to be to placate the implacable? So provocative of animosity, even in the home of learning, is the rivalry of those who pursue different studies or whose opinions differ concerning the studies they pursue in common. However, I care not if "Polydamas and the women of Troy prefer Labeo to me;—a trifle this".

Yet to prevent complete despair, I see here and there, if I do not mistake, some who without a word show clearly by their looks how

*Reprinted from *Milton: Private Correspondence and Academic Exercises,* trans. Phyllis B. Tillyard. London: Cambridge University Press, 1932, pp. 53-64, by permission.

well they wish me. The approval of these, few though they be, is more precious to me than that of the countless hosts of the ignorant, who /54/ lack all intelligence, reasoning power, and sound judgment, and who pride themselves on the ridiculous effervescing froth of their verbiage. Stripped of their covering of patches borrowed from new-fangled authors, they will prove to have no more in them than a serpent's slough, and once they have come to the end of their stock of phrases you will find them unable to utter so much as a syllable, for all the world like dumb men or the frogs of Seriphus. How difficult Heraclitus would find it, were he still alive, to keep a straight face at the sight of these speechifiers (if I may call them so without offence), first grandly spouting their lines in the tragic part of Euripides' Orestes, or as the mad Hercules in his dying agony, and then, their slender stock of phrases exhausted and their glory all gone, drawing in their horns and crawling off like snails.

But to return to the point, from which I have wandered a little. If there is anyone who has refused peace on any terms and declared war *a mort* against me, I will for once stoop to beg and entreat him to lay aside his animosity for a moment and show himself an unbiassed judge in this debate, and not to allow the speaker's fault (if such there be) to prejudice the best and most deserving of causes. If you consider that I have spoken with too much sharpness and bitterness, I confess that I have done so intentionally, for I wish the beginning of my speech to resemble the first gleam of dawn, which presages the fairest day when overcast.

The question whether Day or Night is preferable is no common theme of discussion, and it is now my duty, the task meted out to me this morning, to probe the subject thoroughly and radically, though it might seem better suited to a poetical exercise than to a contest of rhetoric.

Did I say that Night had declared war on Day? What should this portend? What means this daring enterprise? Are the Titans waging anew their ancient war, and renewing the battle of Phlegra's plain? Has Earth /55/ brought forth new offspring of portentous stature to flout the gods of heaven? Or has Typhoeus forced his way from beneath the bulk of Etna piled upon him? Or last, has Briareus eluded Cerberus and escaped from his fetters of adamant? What can it possibly be that has now thrice roused the hopes of the gods of hell to rule the empire of the heavens? Does Night so scorn the thunderbolt of Jove? Cares she nothing for the matchless might of Pallas, which wrought such havoc in days of old among the earth-born brothers? Has she forgotten Bacchus' triumph over the shattered band of Giants, renowned through all the space of heaven? No, none of these. Full well she remembers, to her grief, how of those brothers most were slain by Jove, and the survivors driven in headlong flight even to the furthest corners of the underworld. Not for war, but for something far other, does she now anxiously prepare. Her thoughts now turn to complaints and accusations, and, womanlike, after a brave fight with tooth and nail, she proceeds to argument or rather abuse, to try, I suppose, whether her hands or her tongue are the better weapon. But I will soon show how baseless, how arrogant, and how ill-founded is her claim to supremacy, compared with Day's. And indeed I see Day herself, awakened by the crowing of the cock, hastening hither more swiftly than is her wont, to hear her own praise.

Now since it is generally agreed that to be of noble lineage and to trace one's descent back to kings or gods of old is an essential qualification for honours and dignity, it behoves us to enquire, first, which of the two is of nobler birth, secondly, which can trace back her descent the furthest, and thirdly, which is of the greater service to mankind?

I find it stated by the most ancient authorities on mythology that Demogorgon, the ancestor of all the gods (whom I suppose to be identical with the Chaos of the ancients), was the father of Earth, among his many children. Night was the child of Earth, by an unknown /56/ father, (though Hesiod gives a slightly different pedigree and calls Night the child of Chaos, in the line "From Chaos sprang Erebus and black Night"). Whatever her parentage, when she had reached marriageable age, the shepherd Phanes asked her to wife. Her mother consented, but she herself opposed the match, refusing to contract an alliance with a man she did not know and had never seen, and one moreover whose style of life was so different from her own. Annoyed at the rebuff, and with his love turned to hatred, Phanes in his indignation pursued this dusky daughter of Earth through all the length and breadth of the world to slay her. She now feared his enmity as much as she had previously scorned his love. Therefore she did not feel secure enough even among the most distant peoples or in the most remote places, nor even in the very bosom of her mother, but fled for refuge, secretly and by stealth, to the incestuous embrace of her brother Erebus. Thus she found at once a release from her pressing fears and a husband who was certainly very like herself. From this pretty pair Aether and Day are said to have sprung, according to Hesiod, whom I have already quoted:

> From Night again sprang Aether and the Day
> Whom she conceived and bore by Erebus' embrace.

But the more cultured Muses and Philosophy herself, the neighbour of the gods, forbid us to place entire confidence in the poets who have given the gods their forms, especially the Greek poets; and no one should regard it as a reproach to them that in a question of such importance they hardly seem sufficiently reliable authorities. For if any of them has departed from the truth to some slight extent, the blame should not be laid upon their genius, which is most divine, but upon the perverse and blind ignorance of the age, which at that time was all-pervading. They have attained an ample meed of honour and of glory by gathering together in /57/ one place and forming into organised communities men who previously roamed like beasts at random through the forests and mountains, and by being the first to teach, by their divine inspiration, all the sciences which are known to-day, arraying them in the charming cloak of fable; and their best title to everlasting fame (and that no mean one) is that they have left to their successors the full development of that knowledge of the Arts which they so happily began.

Do not then, whoever you are, hastily accuse me of disregarding and altering the statements of all the ancient poets, without any authority to support me. For I am not taking upon myself to do that, but am only attempting to bring them to the test of reason, and thereby to examine whether they can bear the scrutiny of strict truth.

First, then, the story that makes Night the child of Earth is a learned and elegant allegory of antiquity; for what is it that makes night envelop the world but the dense and solid earth, coming between the sun's light and our horizon?

Then, as to the statements of the mythologists, calling Night sometimes fatherless, sometimes motherless, these too are pleasing fictions, if we understand them to signify that she was a bastard or a changeling, or else that her parents refused for very shame to acknowledge so infamous and ignoble a child. But why they should believe that Phanes, endowed as he was with a wondrous and superhuman beauty, was so much in love with Night, a mere mulatto or silhouette, as even to wish to marry her, seems a problem hopelessly difficult to solve, unless the phenomenal scarcity of females at that time left him no choice.

But now let us come to close quarters with our subject. The ancients interpret Phanes as the sun or the day, and in relating that he at first sought Night in marriage and then pursued her to avenge his rejection, they mean only to signify the alternation of day and /58/ night. But why should they have thought it necessary, in order to show this, to represent Phanes as a suitor for the hand of Night, when their perpetual alternation and mutual repulsion, as it were, could be indicated far better by the figure of an innate and unremitting hatred? for it is well known that light and darkness have been divided from one another by an implacable hatred from the very beginning of time. It is in fact my opinion that Night got her Greek name of εὐφρόνη for the very reason that she showed caution and good sense in refusing to bind herself in wedlock to Phanes; for if she had once submitted to his embrace she would doubtless have been destroyed by his beams and by his unendurable radiance, and either annihilated altogether or utterly consumed by fire; like Semele, who, legend says, perished by fire, against the will of her lover Jove. For this reason, with a proper regard for her security, she preferred Erebus to Phanes. With reference to this, Martial aptly and wittily says, "Worst of husbands, worst of wives, I wonder not that you agree so well".

It is, I think, proper to mention with what a handsome family, how like their mother, she presented her husband—namely Misery, Envy, Fear, Deceit, Fraud, Obstinacy, Poverty, Want, Hunger, Fretfulness, Sickness, Old Age, Pallor, Darkness, Sleep, Death, and Charon, her last child; so that the proverb *tel arbre, tel fruit* is exactly applicable to this case.

There are, however, some who maintain that Night also bore Aether and Day to her husband Erebus. But who in his senses would not howl down and turn out the advocate of such a theory, as he would anyone who seriously propounded Democritus' notions or the fairy-tales of childhood? Is it indeed probable on the face of it that black and gloomy Night should be the mother of a child so comely, so sweet, so universally beloved and desired? Such a child, as soon as conceived, would have caused her mother's death by her birth before due time, would have driven her father Erebus into headlong /59/ flight, and forced old Charon to hide his dazzled eyes beneath the waters of the Styx and flee to seek what refuge he might in the realms below, as fast as his oars and sails could carry him. No, so far from being born in Hades, Day has never even shown her face there, nor can she find entrance even through a chink or cranny, except in defiance of Fate's decree. Nay, I dare rather declare that Day is older than Night, and that when the world had but newly emerged from Chaos, Day shed her wide-spreading rays over it, before ever the turn of Night had come—unless indeed we are so perverse as to call by the name of Night that foul and murky darkness, or regard it as identical with Demogorgon.

Therefore I hold that Day is the eldest daughter of Heaven, or rather of his son, begotten by him, it is said, to be the comfort of the race of men and the terror of the infernal gods, for fear lest Night should rule unopposed, lest Ghosts and Furies and all that loathsome brood of monsters, unchecked by any barrier between Earth and Hades, should leave the pit of Hell and make their way even to the upper world, and lest wretched Man, enveloped and surrounded by murky darkness, should suffer even in this life the tortures of the damned.

So far, Members of the University, I have endeavoured to drag from their deep and dark hiding-places the obscure children of Night; you will immediately perceive how worthy they are of their parentage—especially if I should first devote the best of my small powers to the praise of Day—though Day herself must far transcend the eloquence of all who sing her praise.

In the first place, there is assuredly no need to describe to you how welcome and how desirable Day is to every living thing. Even the birds cannot hide their delight, but leave their nests at peep of dawn and noise it abroad from the tree-tops in sweetest song, or darting upwards as near as they may to the sun, take their flight to welcome the returning day. First of all these the wakeful cock acclaims the sun's coming, and like /60/ a herald bids mankind shake off the bonds of sleep, and rise and run with joy to greet the new-born day. The kids skip in the meadows, and beasts of every kind leap and gambol in delight. The sad heliotrope, who all night long has gazed toward the east, awaiting her beloved Sun, now smiles and beams at her lover's approach. The marigold too and rose, to add their share to the joy of all, open their petals and shed abroad their perfume, which they have kept for the Sun alone, and would not give to Night, shutting themselves up within their little leaves at fall of evening. And all the other flowers raise their heads, drooping and weighed down with dew, and offer themselves to the Sun, mutely begging him to kiss away the tear-drops which his absence brought. The Earth too decks herself in lovelier robes to honour the Sun's coming, and the clouds, arrayed in garb of every hue, attend the rising god in festive train and long procession. And last, that nothing may be lacking to proclaim his praise, the Persians and the Libyans give him divine honours; the Rhodians too have dedicated to his glory that far-famed Colossus of astounding size, created by the miraculous art of Chares of Lindus; to the Sun too, we are told, the Indians even to this day make sacrifice with incense and with every kind of pomp. You yourselves, Members of the University, must bear witness how delightful, how welcome, how long-awaited is the light of morning, since it recalls you to the cultured Muses from whom cruel Night

parted you still unsatisfied and athirst. Saturn, hurled down to Hades
from highest heaven, bears witness how gladly he would return to
the light of day from that dread gloom, would Jove but grant the
boon. Lastly, it is manifest that Pluto himself far preferred light to
his own kingdom of darkness, since he so often strove to gain the
realm of heaven. Thus Orpheus says with truth and with poetic skill
in his hymn to Dawn—"Then of a truth do mortal men rejoice, nor
is there one who flees thy face which shines above, when thou dost
shake /61/ sweet sleep from their eyes. Every man is glad, and every
creeping thing, all the tribes of beast and bird, and all the many
creatures of the deep".

Nor is this to be wondered at, when we reflect that Day serves for
use as well as pleasure, and is alone fitted to further the business of
life; for who would have the hardihood to sail the wide and boundless
seas, without a hope that Day would dawn? He would cross the ocean
even as the ghosts cross Lethe and Acheron, beset on every hand by
the fearsome darkness. Every man would then pass his life in his
own mean hovel, hardly daring even to creep outside, so that the
dissolution of human society must needs follow. To no purpose would
Apelles have pictured Venus rising from the waves, in vain would
Zeuxis have painted Helen, if dark, dense night hid from our eyes
these wondrous sights. In vain too would the earth bring forth in
abundance vines twining in many a winding trail, in vain nobly
towering trees; in vain would she deck herself anew with buds and
blossoms, as with stars, striving to imitate the heaven above. Then
indeed that noblest of the senses, sight, would lose its use to every
creature; yes, and the light of the world's eye being quenched, all
things would fade and perish utterly; nor would the men who dwelt
upon the darkened earth long survive this tragedy, since nothing
would be left to support their life, nor any means of staying the
lapse of all things into the primeval Chaos.

One might continue in this strain with unabating flow, but Day
herself in modesty would not permit the full recital, but would hasten
her downward course toward the sunset to check her advocate's
extravagances. My day is now indeed already drawing to its close, and
will soon give place to night, to prevent your saying in jest that this
is the longest day though the season is midwinter. This alone I ask,
that by your leave I may add a few words which I cannot well omit.

With good reason, then, have the poets declared that /62/ Night
springs from Hell, since by no means whatever could so many grievous
ills descend upon mankind from any other quarter. For when night
falls all things grow foul and vile, no difference can then be seen

between a Helen and Canidia, a precious jewel and a common stone (but that some gems have power to outlive the darkness). Then too the loveliest spots strike horror to the heart, a horror gathering force from a silence deep and sad. All creatures lingering in the fields, be they man or beast, hasten to house or lair for refuge; then, hiding their heads beneath their coverings, they shut their eyes against the dread aspect of Night. None may be seen abroad save thieves and rogues who fear the light, who, breathing murder and rapine, lie in wait to rob honest folk of their goods, and wander forth by night alone, lest day betray them. For Day lays bare all crimes, nor ever suffers wrongdoing to pollute her light. None will you meet save ghosts and spectres, and fearsome goblins who follow in Night's train from the realms below; it is their boast that all night long they rule the earth and share it with mankind. To this end, I think, night sharpens our hearing, that our ears may catch the sooner and our hearts perceive with greater dread the groans of spectres, the screeching of owls and night-birds, and the roaring of lions that prowl in search of prey. Hence clearly is revealed that man's deceit who says that night brings respite from their fears to men and lulls every care to rest. How false and vain is this opinion they know well from their own bitter experience who have ever felt the pangs of guilty consciences; they are beset by Sphinxes and Harpies, Gorgons and Chimaeras, who hunt their victims down with flaming torches in their hands.

Those poor wretches too know it full well who have no friend to help or succour them, none to assuage their grief with words of comfort, but must pour out their useless plaints to senseless stones, longing and praying for the dawn of day. For this reason did that choicest /63/ poet Ovid call Night the mighty foster-mother of cares.

Some indeed say that it is above all by night that our bodies, broken and worn out by the labours of the day, are revived and restored. But this is the merciful ordinance of God, for which we owe no gratitude to Night. But even were it so, sleep is not a thing so precious that Night deserves honour for the bestowal of it. For when we betake ourselves to sleep, we do in truth but confess ourselves poor and feeble creatures, whose puny frames cannot endure even a little while without repose. And, to be sure, what is sleep but the image and semblance of death? Hence in Homer Sleep and Death are twins, conceived together and born at a single birth.

Lastly, it is thanks to the sun that the moon and the other stars display their fires by night, for they have no light to radiate but such as they borrow from the sun.

Who then but a son of darkness, a robber, a gamester, or one whose wont it is to spend his nights in the company of harlots and snore away his days—who, I ask, but such a fellow would have undertaken to defend a cause so odious and discreditable? I wonder that he dare so much as look upon this sun, or share with other men, without a qualm, that light which he is slandering so ungratefully. He deserves to share the fate of Python, slain by the stroke of the sun's hostile rays. He deserves to pass a long and loathsome life imprisoned in Cimmerian darkness. He deserves, above all, to see sleep overcoming his hearers even as he speaks, so that his best eloquence affects them no more than an idle dream, till, drowsy himself, he is cheated into taking his hearers' nods and snores for nods of approval and murmurs of praise as he ends his speech.

But I see the black brows of Night, and note the advance of darkness; I must withdraw, lest Night overtake me unawares.

I beg you then, my hearers, since Night is but the passing and the death of Day, not to give Death the /64/ preference over Life, but graciously to honour my cause with your votes; so may the Muses prosper your studies, and Dawn, the friend of the Muses, hear your prayers; and may the Sun, who sees and hears all things, hearken to all in this assembly who honour and support his cause. I have done.

Samuel Johnson

From Milton*

Of the two pieces, *L'Allegro* and *Il Penseroso*, I believe, opinion is uniform; every man that reads them, reads them with pleasure. The author's design is not, what Theobald has remarked, merely to shew how objects derive their colours from the mind, by representing the operation of the same things upon the gay and the melancholy temper, or upon the same man as he is differently disposed; but rather how, among the successive variety of appearances, every disposition of mind takes hold on those by which it may be gratified.

The *cheerful* man hears the lark in the morning; the *pensive* man hears the nightingale in the evening. The *cheerful* man sees the cock strut, and hears the horn and hounds echo in the wood; then walks, *not unseen*, to observe the glory of the rising sun, or listen to the singing milk-maid, and view the labours of the plowman and the mower; then casts his eyes about him over scenes of smiling plenty, and looks up to the distant tower, the residence of some fair /159/ inhabitant; thus he pursues real gaiety through a day of labour or of play, and delights himself at night with the fanciful narratives of superstitious ignorance.

The *pensive* man, at one time, walks *unseen* to muse at midnight; and at another hears the sullen curfew. If the weather drives him home, he sits in a room lighted only by *glowing embers*; or by a lonely lamp outwatches the north star, to discover the habitation of separate souls, and varies the shades of meditation, by contemplating the magnificent or pathetic scenes of tragick and epick poetry.

---

*Reprinted from Samuel Johnson, *The Lives of the Most Eminent English Poets: With Critical Observations on Their Works*. Edinburgh: Peter Hill, 1815, I, 158-160. Johnson published his *Lives* in 1779 and 1781.

When the morning comes, a morning gloomy with rain and wind, he walks into the dark trackless woods, falls asleep by some murmuring water, and with melancholy enthusiasm expects some dream of prognostication, or some music played by aërial performers.

Both Mirth and Melancholy are solitary, silent inhabitants of the breast, that neither receive nor transmit communication; no mention is therefore made of a philosophical friend, or a pleasant companion. The seriousness does not arise from any participation of calamity, nor the gaiety from the pleasures of the bottle.

The man of *cheerfulness,* having exhausted the country, tries what *towered cities* will afford, and mingles with scenes of splendour, gay assemblies, and nuptial festivities; but he mingles a mere spectator, as, when the learned comedies of Jonson, or the wild dramas of Shakespeare, are exhibited, he attends the theatre.

The *pensive* man never loses himself in crowds, but walks the cloister, or frequents the cathedral. Milton probably had not yet forsaken the church.

Both his characters delight in musick; but he seems to think that cheerful notes would have obtained from Pluto a complete dismission of Eurydice, of whom solemn sounds only procured a conditional release. /160/

For the old age of Cheerfulness he makes no provision; but Melancholy he conducts with great dignity to the close of life. His Cheerfulness is without levity, and his Pensiveness without asperity.

Through these two poems the images are properly selected and nicely distinguished; but the colours of the diction seem not sufficiently discriminated. I know not whether the characters are kept sufficiently apart. No mirth can, indeed, be found in his melancholy; but I am afraid that I always meet some melancholy in his mirth. They are two noble efforts of imagination.

Thomas Warton

Notes on Milton's
Companion Poems*

L'Allegro and *Il Penseroso* may be called the two first descriptive
poems in the English language. It is perhaps true, that the characters
are not sufficiently kept apart. But this circumstance has been productive of greater excellencies. It has been remarked, "No mirth indeed
can be found in his melancholy, but I am afraid I always meet some
melancholy in his mirth." Milton's is the dignity of mirth. His
cheerfulness is the cheerfulness of gravity. The objects he selects in
his *L'Allegro* are so far gay, as they do not naturally excite sadness.
Laughter and jollity are named only as personifications, and never
exemplified. *Quips* and *Cranks*, /97/ and *wanton wiles*, are enumerated
only in general terms. There is specifically no mirth in contemplating
a fine landscape. And even his landscape, although it has flowery
meads and flocks, wears a shade of pensiveness; and contains *russet*
lawns, fallows *gray*, and *barren* mountains, overhung with *labouring*
clouds. Its old turreted mansion peeping from the trees, awakens
only a train of solemn and romantic, perhaps melancholy, reflection.
Many a pensive man listens with delight to the milkmaid *singing
blithe*, to the mower *whetting his seythe*, and to a distant peal of
village bells. He chose such illustrations as minister matter for true
poetry, and genuine description. Even his most brilliant imagery is
mellowed with the sober hues of philosophic meditation. It was
impossible for the author of *Il Penseroso* to be more cheerful, or to
paint mirth with levity; that is, otherwise than in the colours of the

---

*Reprinted from Thomas Warton, editor, *Poems upon Several Occasions, English,
Italian, and Latin, with Translations,* by John Milton. London: G. G. J. and
J. Robinson, 1791, pp. 96-97. Spelling has been modernized by the editors.

higher poetry. Both poems are the result of the same feelings, and the same habits of thought.

Doctor Johnson has remarked, that in *L'Allegro*, "no part of the gaiety is made to arise from the pleasures of the bottle." The truth is, that Milton means to describe the cheerfulness of the philosopher or the student, the amusements of a contemplative mind. And on this principle, he seems unwilling to allow, that Mirth is the offspring of Bacchus and Venus, deities who preside over sensual gratifications; but rather adopts the fiction of those more serious and sapient fablers, who suppose, that her proper parents are Zephyr and Aurora: intimating, that his cheerful enjoyments are those of the temperate and innocent kind, of early hours and rural pleasures. That critic does not appear to have entered into the spirit, or to have comprehended the meaning, of our author's *Allegro*.

No man was ever so disqualified to turn Puritan as Milton. In both these poems, he professes himself to be highly pleased with the choral church music, with Gothic cloisters, the painted windows and vaulted aisles of a venerable cathedral, with tilts and tournaments, and with masques and pageantries. What very repugnant and unpoetical principles did he afterwards adopt! He helped to subvert monarchy, to destroy subordination, and to level all distinctions of rank. But this scheme was totally inconsistent with the splendours of society, with *throngs of knights and barons bold*, with *store of ladies*, and *high triumphs*, which belonged to a court. *Pomp*, and *feast*, and *revelry*, the show of Hymen, *with mask and antique pageantry*, were among the state and trappings of nobility, which he detested as an advocate for republicanism. His system of worship, which renounced all outward solemnity, all that had ever any connection with popery, tended to overthrow the *studious cloisters pale*, and the *high embowed* roof; to remove the *storied windows richly dight*, and to silence the *pealing organ* and the *full-voiced quire*. The delights arising from these objects were to be sacrificed to the cold and philosophical spirit of Calvinism, which furnished no pleasures to the imagination.

Lawrence Babb

From The Background of "Il Penseroso"*

I

Among the four temperaments which Renaissance physiology and psychology describe, the melancholic is the most unfortunate. Black bile, the melancholic humor, is normally cold, dry, heavy, and black. It therefore causes fear and sorrow, emotions which Renaissance psychology associates with coldness and dryness; its sluggish inertia produces torpor of body and mind; very often, either by vapors which rise from it or by its own substance, it discolors the physical instruments of perception and thought so that all the images in the brain are black and funereal.

Melancholy men

> are moste parte sad, throughe their melancoly spirites,[1] troublous and darke . . . they talk litle . . . they couet alwaie to be alone . . . throughe melancolye fumes they haue horrible dreames . . . they thinke nothing sure, they alwey drede, through darkenes of theyr spirites.[2]

They become "ill fauored, leane, dry, lank, pylde skinned . . . the face . . . pale, yelowyshe & swarty."[3] Their "melancholie causeth dulnesse of conceit,"[4] and they are

---

*Reprinted from *Studies in Philology*, XXXVII (April, 1940), 257-273, by permission.
[1]The *animal spirits* are subtle fluids which are supposed to flow through the nerves and to serve as mediums of communication between the brain and the organs of sense and motion.
[2]*Regimen Sanitatis Salerni*, tr. Thomas Paynell (London, 1575), fol. cxliii.
[3]Levinus Lemnius, *The Touchstone of Complexions*, tr. Thomas Newton (London, 1576), fol. 146r.
[4]Timothy Bright, *A Treatise of Melancholie* (London, 1586), p. 129.

altogether grosse and slacke in all their actions both of bodie and
minde, fearefull, sluggish, and without vnderstanding.[5]

The condition of such a man is not considered pathological. His
peculiarities are due simply to a moderate preponderance of black
bile, just as the sanguine man's energy and cheerfulness are due to a
/258/ moderate abundance of blood. Sometimes, however, because of
bad diet, physical illness, or mental perturbation, the melancholy
humor abounds beyond the rather vague limits of normality and
engenders mental disease. There is, furthermore, an "unnatural"
melancholy, or "adust" melancholy, a noxious black humor produced
when abnormal heat burns a natural humor. This adust humor
disorders the mind even more than natural black bile.

Terror, despair, and misanthropy are the primary symptoms in
most melancholic mental disorders.[6] A man deranged by melancholy is

alwaies fearefull and trembling, in such sort as that he is afraid
of euery thing, yea and maketh himselfe a terrour vnto himselfe,
as the beast which looketh himselfe in a glasse . . . with an
vnseparable sadnes, which oftentimes turneth into dispayre . . .
[in sleep] hee is assayled with a thousand vaine visions, and
hideous buggards . . . he can not liue with companie. To conclude,
hee is become a sauadge creature, haunting the shadowed places,
suspicious, solitarie, enemie to the Sunne, and one whom nothing
can please, but onely disconcentment, which forgeth vnto it selfe
a thousand false and vaine imaginations.[7]

Melancholy

causeth men to be aliened from the nature of man, and wholly
to discard themselves from all society . . . to live in grots, caves,
and other hidden cels of the earth.[8]

---

[5]André Du Laurens, *A Discourse of the Preservation of the Sight*, tr. Richard
Surphlet (London, 1599), pp. 85-86 (Shakespeare Association Facsimiles, No. 15).

[6]The scientific writers, however, occasionally distinguish odd varieties. There are
a laughing melancholy and a furious melancholy, due respectively to burned blood
and choler; see Bright, *Treatise*, pp. 110-11, and Robert Burton, *The Anatomy of
Melancholy*, ed. A. R. Shilleto (London, 1926-27), I, 197-99. Lemnius describes an
early stage of exhileration and a later stage of depression in adust melancholic
disorders (*Touchstone*, fols. 147-48).

[7]Du Laurens, *Discourse*, p. 82.

[8]Thomas Walkington, *The Optick Glasse of Humors* (London, 1639), p. 132. This
work was first published in 1607.

[It] maketh men . . . Haters of the light, delighting onely like the
Shrieke Owle or the Bitterne in desolate places, and monuments
of the dead.⁹. . . /260/

Various English moralists endeavor anxiously to make it clear that
melancholy and godliness have nothing in common. The Rev. Richard
Greenham attributes a friend's lamentable condition of spirit "partly
[to] Melancholy, partly [to] Sathan working therewith."¹⁶ Samuel
Hieron¹⁷ and John Sedgwick,¹⁸ both ministers, distinguish carefully
between melancholy depression of mind and true repentance. Robert
Crofts distinguishes melancholic fear from the pious fear of doing evil.
Melancholy fear, he says, causes distrust even of divine Providence.¹⁹

John Harvey, English physician, asserts that he is not "so melan-
cholique" as to credit melancholy men with prophetic powers,²⁰ and
Henry Howard, Earl of Northampton, says that "sooner shall a man
finde out a pure virgin in Sodome, then a true Prophete in the caue
of melancholy."²¹

Melancholy, then, makes men dull and blockish, fearful and sorrow-
ful without apparent cause, fond of solitude and darkness, subject to
the most terrifying and ridiculous illusions. Melancholy men are often
wretched creatures who have fallen to the level of beasts and who
have lost the privilege of communion with heaven.

Greek medicine, especially the medical system of Galen,* is the
ultimate source of this group of ideas. /261/

II

One discovers, however, a second and a very different conception
of melancholia in learned works of the Renaissance, a conception of
considerably greater dignity. This also has a classical source.

---

⁹Edward Reynolds, *A Treatise of the Faculties and Passions of the Soule of Man*
(London, 1640), p. 130.

¹⁶*Works* (London, 1599), p. 450.

¹⁷*Davids Penitentiall Psalme Opened* (Cambridge, 1617), pp. 258-59. *Cf.* Bright,
Treatise, pp. 187-98.

¹⁸*The Bearing and Burden of the Spirit* (London, 1640), pp. 115-23.

¹⁹*Paradise Within Us* (London, 1640), pp. 113-16. *Cf.* Bright, *Treatise*, p. 202, and
Burton, *Anatomy*, I, 444; III, 452 ff.

²⁰*A Discoursive Probleme Concerning Prophecies* (London, 1588), p. 4.

²¹*A Defensative Against the Poyson of Supposed Prophecies* (London, 1583),
fol. Iiiiʳ.

*[Original article carried footnote 22 here. *Ed.*]

A problem of Aristotle's[23] which greatly interested Renaissance scholars begins with the question:

> Why is it that all those who have become eminent in philosophy or politics or poetry or the arts are clearly of an atrabilious temperament . . . ?

Many of the great heroes of Greece, says the writer, were melancholic; Heracles, Ajax and Bellerophon, all of whom went mad, are his examples. The great thinkers Empedocles, Socrates, and Plato, he says, also were atrabilious.

The answer which he gives would be much more to the point if his question had been: Why does black bile have such diverse effects upon temperament? This humor, he says, has the capability of varying in temperature from extreme heat to extreme cold and therefore produces, in one instance or another, all the various traits of personality which arise from internal heat or cold (as, in his opinion, most do). Cold melancholy causes torpidity and despondency; hot melancholy causes madness.

> Many too, if this heat approaches the region of the intellect, are affected by diseases of frenzy and possession; and this is the origin of Sibyls and soothsayers and all inspired persons, when they are affected not by disease but by natural temperament. Maracus, the Syracusan, was actually a better poet when he was out of his mind.

When black bile has "a mean temperature" it produces a condition admirably adapted to intellectual activity. It makes men "cleverer and less eccentric and in many respects superior to others either in mental accomplishments or in the arts or in public life." Men who are only moderately atrabilious—those who "possess a mixed temperament"—"are men of genius."

Renaissance scholars find authoritative confirmation for these ideas, they believe, in Plato's statement that the poet must be /262/ touched with madness[24] and in Democritus' opinion that true poetry is written

---

[23]*Problemata*, XXX, i. I have used the translation of E. S. Forster in vol. VII of *The Works of Aristotle* (Oxford, 1908-31). There is considerable doubt as to the genuineness of the *Problemata*. Cicero and Plutarch, however, believed that the passage under consideration was Aristotle's; see *Tusculanae Disputationes*, I, 33; *De Divinatione*, I, 38; *Lysander*, 2.

[24]*Phaedrus*, 245.

in a delirium of divine origin.[25] Neither Plato nor Democritus, however, says anything about melancholy in connection with poetic genius. ⌞Many Renaissance writers, fortified by these authorities, assert that melancholy fosters intellectual and imaginative powers.⌟ Most of them see clearly how paradoxical it is to say this of the humor which, as they readily admit, causes so much stupidity and absurdity. They consequently busy themselves with explanations (for Aristotle's explanation does not really explain) and offer a diversity of opinions. They name this or that variety of black bile as the one which Aristotle meant. They say that black bile must be qualified by intermixture with other humors. Many of them adopt Aristotle's idea that melancholy must be moderately hot if it is to heighten the mental powers.[26]

Frequently they call to their assistance an aphorism of Heraclitus': "Dry light is the wisest and best soul."[27] All melancholy is dry. It is supposed to shine when it is hot. Thus it is possible to assume that "Dry light" means hot melancholy. Two principles of Renaissance psychology are that dryness aids the intellect and that heat aids the imagination.[28] Hot melancholy, then, should foster both intellectual and imaginative abilities. The psychologists seldom forget, however, that Aristotle specifies moderate heat.

Marcilio Ficino, Florentine humanist, philosopher, and physician, has a great deal to say about the relation between melancholy and the mental faculties in *De Studiosorum Sanitate Tuenda*,[29] a /263/ treatise presenting a regimen of living for scholars. Ficino believes, as all Renaissance physicians do, that the scholar's sedentary life and arduous mental endeavor breed the melancholic humor, which in turn engenders the various diseases of body and mind generally attributed to it. All men of letters are melancholy: "Musarum sacerdotes melancholici uel [sunt] ab initio, uel studio [fiunt]."[30] Yet this fact is not altogether unfortunate, for, says Ficino, Aristotle, Plato, and Democritus attribute great excellence to melancholy minds.

[25]See Hermann Diels, *Die Fragmente der Vorsokratiker* (Berlin, 1934-35), II, 146.

[26]If a writer specifies natural melancholy (normally very cold) as the beneficent humor, he usually explains that it must be heated by intermixture with blood or with blood and choler (both warm humors). Unnatural melancholy, of course, may be hot—even too hot—without intermixture with other humors.

[27]*Heracleitus on the Universe*, tr. W. H. S. Jones (London-New York, 1931), p. 495.

[28]See Juan Huarte, *Examen de Ingenios*, tr. R. Carew (London, 1594), pp. 59, 63-64, and Pierre Charron, *Of Wisdome*, tr. Samson Lennard (London, c. 1607), p. 48.

[29]This is the first book of *De Vita Libri Tres*, originally published 1482-89. I have used an edition of Basel, 1549.

[30]P. 14.

If natural melancholy is properly mixed with warmer humors,[31] it is
kindled—without burning—and shines brilliantly. "Huc tendit illud
Heracliti: Lux sicca, anima sapientissima."[32] Ficino describes this
tempered melancholy lyrically. Its color is like that of gold, tinged
with purple. . . . /267/

The Renaissance, then, held simultaneously two conceptions of
melancholia. According to Galenic tradition, melancholia is a most
ignominious and miserable condition of mind; according to the
Aristotelian tradition, it is a most admirable and enviable condition
of mind. These two conceptions are hopelessly intertangled in Renaissance thought and literature. Sometimes they seem at least partially
reconciled through the nice distinctions of the psychologists; sometimes they seem very much at war with each other.[57]

There would have been no such duality, it may be noted, if there
had been no Aristotelian problem, for this problem was the source
of the idea that melancholy men are extraordinarily endowed. If
Renaissance scholars knew of any other classical source for this idea,
they were strangely silent about it.[58] Virtually the whole weight of
classical and medieval medical opinion was against the idea. No
less overpowering an authority than Aristotle's could have given it
currency./268/

If there had been no Aristotelian problem, the melancholic attitude would never have won the popularity that it enjoyed during the
Renaissance. No man would have cared to confess himself melancholy
if that had been to confess himself blockish and silly. But Aristotle
lent melancholia a philosophic glamor, and many men were willing
and eager to confess themselves affected. Thus arose the vogue of
melancholy in Italy,[59] and from Italy it spread to England.[60] Melancholy men, most of them belonging to the "malcontent" type, were
numerous in England during the late sixteenth and early seventeenth
centuries and were doubtless responsible for England's great interest
in melancholy. Englishmen would probably have been interested in

---

[31]Ficino gives the exact proportions (p. 17): eight parts of blood, two of yellow
bile, and two of black bile. This formula is repeated by Baptista Porta, *De Humana
Physiognomonia* (Oberusel, 1601), p. 23.

[32]P. 18.

[57]Du Bosc's essay, quoted above, presents first the evil effects of the melancholic
humor and then the good effects. The two halves of the essay flatly contradict each
other.

[58]Plato and Democritus do not actually mention melancholy. Cicero and Plutarch
(see footnote 23) cite Aristotle as authority.

[59]See Erwin Panofsky and Fritz Saxl, *Dürers "Melencolia I": eine Quellen- und
Typen-Geschichtliche Untersuchung* (Leipzig-Berlin, 1923), Kap. III.

[60]See Zera S. Fink, "Jaques and the Malcontent Traveler," *PQ, XIV* (1935), 237-52.

psychopathology in any case, but if they had seen melancholy men less frequently, they might have given no more attention to melancholy than to madness, frenzy, or idiocy. Aristotle's problem was the remote cause of the melancholy men of Elizabethan and early Stuart drama, satire, and character sketches.

The Galenic conception is the dominant conception in Renaissance medical works. The Aristotelian conception, however, is of much greater interest to the student of literature.

III

Both conceptions of melancholy are amply represented, of course, in Elizabethan and early Stuart literature. Each to some extent colors the other. Two illustrations drawn from the seventeenth century characters will show the contrast.

The melancholy man in the Overbury collection is a highly disagreeable and unsociable person, seldom

> found without the shade of some grove, in whose bottome a river dwels. Hee carries a cloud in his face, never faire weather. . . . His spirits, and the sunne are enemies; the sunne bright and warme, his humour blacke and cold: variety of foolish apparitions people his head . . . [his fantasies] are the consuming evils, and evill consumptions that consume him alive. Lastly, he is a man onely in shew, but comes short of the better part; /269/ a whole reasonable soule, which is mans chiefe pre-eminence, and sole marke from creatures sensible.[61]

Wye Saltonstall's melancholy man

> Is a full vessell which makes not so great a sound, as those that are more empty and answer to every knocke. . . . Hee can be merry without expressing it by an ignorant laughter. . . . If he walke and see you not, 'tis because his mind [is] busied in some serious contemplation . . . [He] contemnes a gaudy outside as the badge of fooles. He goes therefore commonly in blacke, his Hat unbrusht, a hasty gate with a looke fixt on the ground, as though he were looking pins there, when yet his mind is then soaring in some high contemplation; and is then alwayes most busy, when hee seemes most idle.[62]

---

[61]*The Miscellaneous Works in Prose and Verse of Sir Thomas Overbury, Knt.*, ed. Edward F. Rimbault (London, 1586), pp. 73-74. The phrase "creatures sensible" means "beasts."

[62]*Picturae Loquentes* (London, 1631), No. 8.

Melancholy in religious poetry is of especial importance to the present study. Ben Jonson seems to think that melancholy and true religious feeling can have no relation:

> Good, and great God, can I not thinke of thee,
> But it must, straight, my melancholy bee?
> Is it interpreted in me disease,
> That, laden with my sinnes, I seeke for ease? [63]

To John Donne, however, melancholy and piety seem naturally associated:

> *Deigne at my hands this crown of prayer and praise,*
> Weav'd in my low devout melancholie . . .[64]

An anonymous poet of the early Stuart period bids farewell to the "guilded follies" of the world and determines to live apart from mankind in "an holy melancholy."[65] James Day, in a poem called "The Melancholicke Soules comfort," writes that no music is more acceptable to the Lord than "*sobs and cries.*"[66] Humphrey Mill expresses his religious feeling in a volume called *Poems Occasioned /270/ by a Melancholy Vision.*[67] On the title-page appears the motto "His gaudit musa tenebris." Henry Vaughan addresses Christ:

> Fair and yong light! my guide to holy
> Grief and soul-curing melancholy . . .[68]

IV

No two literary pieces could better illustrate the dualism of the concept *melancholy* as it existed in the Carolinian period than "L'Allegro" and "Il Penseroso." In the first, melancholy is associated with hell and midnight, with "horrid shapes, and shrieks, and sights unholy"; is banished to an "uncouth cell" in a dark and forbidding desert; is rejected as utterly loathsome. Milton is exorcising the crucifying melancholy madness of the Galenic tradition. In "Il Penseroso,"

---

[63]"To Heaven," *The Forrest*, p. 840 (Facsimile Text Society reprint).
[64]*The Poems of John Donne*, ed. H. J. C. Grierson (Oxford, 1912), I, 318.
[65]Grierson prints this as a spurious Donne lyric (*Poems*, I, 465-67). It appears in Walton's *Complete Angler* (Part I, Chap. XXI).
[66]*A New Spring of Divine Poetrie* (London, 1637), p. 25.
[67]London, 1639.
[68]*The Works of Henry Vaughan*, ed. L. C. Martin (Oxford, 1914), II, 513.

on the other hand, the poet personifies melancholy as a "pensive Nun" of sober and stately beauty, a "Goddess, sage and holy, . . . divinest Melancholy,"[69] and he invites her to be his companion and the ruling influence of his life. This is melancholy in the tradition of Aristotle and Ficino. The melancholy which Milton rejects in "L'Allegro" is not the same thing at all as that which he accepts in "Il Penseroso."

The melancholy of "Il Penseroso" is a melancholy of sober and solitary contemplative pleasures. The goddess herself moves

> With even step and musing gait,
> And looks commercing with the skies.   (38-39)

She is asked to bring with her "calm Peace and Quiet" (45) and

> retirèd Leisure,
> That in trim gardens takes his pleasure
> • • •
> And the mute Silence hist along,
> 'Less Philomel will deign a song.   (49-56)

Under the goddess' influence, the poet will take solitary nocturnal walks

> On the dry smooth-shaven green,
> To behold the wandering moon.   (66-67)

/271/ Or he will sit alone within doors before the glowing embers, "Far from all resort of mirth" (81).

His life will be scholarly; he will "walk the studious cloister's pale" (156). He will apply himself to the study of mystical and divine philosophy:

> let my lamp at midnight hour
> Be seen in some high lonely tower,
> Where I may oft outwatch the Bear,
> With thrice great Hermes, or unsphere
> The spirit of Plato . . .   (85-89)

He will be interested in the arts: in tragedy, in poetry, in sad or solemn music like the song of the nightingale or the clear anthems of

---

[69]She is, appropriately, Saturn's daughter, and she is fittingly dressed in black, "staid Wisdom's hue."

"the pealing organ" and "the full-voiced choir" (161-62). For "Spare Fast," the companion of Melancholy,[70]

> oft with gods doth diet,
> And hears the Muses in a ring
> Aye round about Jove's altar sing.   (46-48)

Most significant of all, Melancholy will encourage the contemplation of divine truth. She is a "Goddess, sage and holy" with

> looks commercing with the skies,
> Thy rapt soul sitting in thine eyes:
> There held in holy passion still,
> Forget thyself to marble . . .   (39-42)

The poet asks her "first and chiefest" to bring with her

> Him that yon soars on golden wing,
> Guiding the fiery-wheelèd throne,
> The Cherub Contemplation.   (52-54)

He looks forward to an old age spent as a religious recluse, to "The hairy gown and mossy cell" (169). He has his canny doubts about melancholic powers of prophecy; but he believes that, through "old experience," he will

>   attain
> To something like prophetic strain.   (173-74)

---

[70]Fasting engenders black bile. See Burton, *Anatomy* I, 263-64; III, 393-96.

J. B. Leishman

From *L'Allegro* and *Il Penseroso* in their Relation to Seventeenth – Century Poetry*

I

My only reason for not describing *L'Allegro* and *Il Penseroso* as the most typically seventeenth-century of Milton's shorter poems is that I cannot conceive how any other seventeenth-century poet could possibly have written them. What, though, may be safely asserted is that many of the most delightful characteristics of seventeenth-century poetry in general are there more perfectly exhibited than elsewhere.

It is not an accident that they are written in that octosyllabic couplet which various poets of the earlier seventeenth century brought to perfection: it was precisely the right form both for Milton's subject-matter and for his attitude towards it; and both subject-matter and attitude (or tone) are here further from Spenser (who never used this metre) and nearer to some of the best seventeenth-century poets than anywhere else in what may be called Milton's major minor poems. There is more wit here than elsewhere in his serious poetry—wit, not in the narrower sense of ingeniousness and the devising of ingenious analogies and comparisons (although there are some traces of this), but wit in the wider sense, as denoting a certain flexibility of mind and mood, a certain balance between seriousness and light-heartedness.

There is also some trace in them of that dialectical, argumentative, and debating strain which is so strong in Donne and in some of his successors.

*Reprinted from *Essays and Studies 1951*, n. s., IV (1951), 1-36, published for the English Association by Messrs. John Murray Ltd., and reprinted by Messrs. Wm. DAWSON & SONS. Reprinted by permission of the publisher and the executor of the author's estate.

How strong is this debating strain, and what exactly is the debate about? Most of us, I suppose, have always assumed that it was about Mirth and Melancholy, but Dr. Tillyard, partly perhaps because he was looking for evidence to support his belief that the two poems, because they do not appear in the Trinity College Manuscript, must have been written before Milton left Cambridge, has declared that they grew out of Milton's *First Prolusion*, a semi-serious academic exercise, delivered not later than July 1628, on the subject "Whether Day or Night is the more /2/ excellent". Noticing, in his lecture[1] on the two poems, Dr. Johnson's objection that the cheerful man and the meditative man are too much alike, Dr. Tillyard declares: /3/

> Nevertheless, the two poems *are* sharply contrasted, and the contrast is that between day and night. *L'Allegro* written in praise of day corresponds to the *First Prolusion*; *Il Penseroso* written in praise of night corresponds to what Milton would have said had he been called to take the other side.

To this it may be shortly replied that *L'Allegro* cannot be described either as a poem about day or as a poem in praise of day, and the *Il Penseroso* cannot be described either as a poem about night or as a poem in praise of night. In each poem, as Warton observed long ago, there is a day piece and a night piece; both the cheerful man and the pensive man have their characteristic day-time and their characteristic evening pleasures, although, as might be expected, in *L'Allegro* it is the day-time and in *Il Penseroso* the evening pleasures that preponderate; and while the list of pleasures in *L'Allegro* begins at dawn, with the lark, that in *Il Penseroso* begins at night, with the nightingale. L'Allegro's evening pleasures begin after the rustic company have heard tales of Robin Goodfellow and gone to bed: he then goes to town ("Towred Cities please us then, And the busie humm of men"), sees tournaments, masques and comedies and hears soft Lydian airs. And just as L'Allegro has his evening pleasures, Il Penseroso has his day-time ones: his dawn is ushered in by a shower; he

---

[1] Published by the English Association, July 1932, and reprinted in *The Miltonic Setting*, 1938. Dr. Tillyard believed that the two poems had been written in the summer of 1631, during Milton's last Long Vacation. More recently Mr. F. W. Bateson (*English Poetry*, 1950, pp. 155-6) has argued (unconvincingly, as it seems to me) in favour of a still earlier date, and would persuade us that the two poems preceded the Nativity Ode and were written during the late summer or autumn of 1629.

goes for a solitary walk in the woods; meditates, sleeps and dreams beside a stream, paces the studious cloister, hears organ and choir in a cathedral or in a college chapel. If, then, there is a contrast between the two poems, it is not that between day and night, and if there is a debate, it is not on the respective merits of day and night. In spite of Dr. Tillyard, we may be content to believe that when Milton exorcised Melancholy and invoked Mirth he supposed himself to be writing a poem about Mirth; that when he exorcised Mirth and invoked Melancholy he supposed himself to be writing a poem about Melancholy; and that mirth and melancholy did not mean precisely the same to him, in spite of Dr. Johnson's complaint that the two characters were not kept sufficiently apart.

The question, what exactly did Milton mean by melancholy? is complex and interesting and will detain us for some time. First, though, it is worth observing that for the idea of two contrasted poems, one praising the pleasures of mirth and the other praising the pleasures of /4/ melancholy, there existed far better and more obvious precedent than his own early prolusion on the superiority of day to night. It was, I think, Sympson, one of the co-editors of the edition of Beaumont and Fletcher's plays published in 1750, who was the first to point out certain obvious resemblances between *Il Penseroso* and Fletcher's song in *The Nice Valour* beginning "Hence, all you vaine Delights". Both play and song were first printed in the folio of 1647, but long before that date the song had become very popular, and it appears in several manuscript collections from about 1620 onwards. In one of these, MS. Malone 21 in the Bodleian, it is followed by a reply entitled *Against Melancholy* and ascribed to "Dr. Strode", that is, to William Strode (1602-1645), Canon of Christ Church, Chaplain to Bishop Corbet, and Public Orator at Oxford. Both Fletcher's poem and Strode's reply to it were printed in the Miscellanies *Wits Interpreter* (1655) and *Wit Restor'd* (1658).

After having dismissed, rather summarily perhaps, Dr. Tillyard's hypothesis, I rather hesitate to advance one of my own. I will, though, venture to suggest that someone may have shown Milton a manuscript of Fletcher's poem and Strode's reply and that this may have started him off. This hypothesis has four great merits: it is simple; it conflicts with no existing facts; it involves no new interpretation of Milton's poems; no one can prove that it is untrue.

Let us, before proceeding, have the two poems before us. Here is Fletcher's:

Hence, all you vaine Delights,
As short as are the nights,
   Wherein you spend your folly.
Ther's nought in this life sweet,
If man were wise to see 't,
   But onely Melancholy,
   O sweetest melancholy.
Welcome, folded Armes and fixed eyes,
A sigh that piercing mortifies,
A look that's fastned to the ground,
A tongue chain'd up without a sound.

Fountaine heads, and pathlesse Groves,
Places which pale passion loves:
Moon-light walkes, when all the fowles
Are warmly hous'd, save Bats and Owles;
   A mid-night Bell, a parting groane,
   These are the sounds we feed upon;
Then stretch our bones in a still gloomy valley,
Nothing's so daintie sweet as lovely melancholy.

/5/ Strode's reply, though not without merit, is far less memorable and distinguished. It is also less romantic and less pictorial than Fletcher's poem, and nearer to some of Jonson's more epigrammatic lyrics.

Returne my joyes and hither bring
A heart not taught to speak but sing,
A jolly spleen, an inward feast,
A causelesse laugh without a jest;
A face which gladnesse doth anoint,
An arme for joy flung out of joynt;
A sprightfull gate that leaves no print,
And makes a feather of a flint;
A heart that's lighter then the aire,
An eye still daunceing in its spheare;
Strong mirth which nothing can controule,
A body nimbler than a Soule;
Free wandring thoughts not ty'de to muse,
Which thinke on all things, nothing choose,
Which ere wee see them come are gone:
These life itselfe doth live upon.
   Then take no care, but only to be jolly:
   To be more wretched then we must is folly.

I may, perhaps, be too confident in my hypothesis, but it seems to me almost self-evident that it was Fletcher's

> Hence, all you vaine Delights

which suggested

> Hence vain deluding joyes

and the rest of the elaborate abjuration at the beginning of *Il Penseroso*, and that it was Strode's catalogue of the qualities which his returning joys were to bring with them which suggested the various personified qualities and moods which Mirth and Melancholy are exhorted to bring with them in Milton's poems. It also seems to me that the luxurious, or, as a seventeenth-century writer might have called it, the humorous and self-pleasing, the on the whole very agreeable, melancholy of Fletcher's poem is much like the kind of melancholy which Milton invokes and describes in *Il Penseroso*, as distinct from the kind which he abjures at the beginning of *L'Allegro*.

There is a further and rather important resemblance between Milton's poems and the pair which I think may have suggested them. Fletcher and Strode do not *argue* as Donne would have done had he chosen to /6/ exert himself upon this topic; they merely *describe*. Fletcher says in effect: "Melancholy's a delicious thing: feel, look, listen"; Strode says in effect: "Mirth's the thing I want — makes you feel like this". This is very different from Donne's method, when, in *The Anagram*, he sets himself to persuade an imaginary friend that it is in all respects better and wiser to marry an old and ugly woman than a young and handsome one, or when he argues with an imaginary mistress that she is refusing to him what she has permitted to a flea. There is *something* of argument, of debate, of paradox, of hyperbole in these poems of Fletcher and Strode and Milton, but not that mock-serious application of close and ingenious argument to the maintenance of monstrously absurd paradox which we often find in Donne. Their poems are also, though far from solemn, more serious than those two of Donne's which I have mentioned. They take their subject more seriously and they treat it more seriously; their subject, one may say, *means* more to them. Milton's poems, as I need scarcely insist, are more serious and elaborate and important than those of Fletcher and Strode, which, in comparison, are almost trifles; nevertheless, Milton's poems too are, partly at least, in the same tradition, the same fashion, the fashion of serious, and yet at the same time light-hearted, poetical debate.

There is indeed a relation between Milton's First Prolusion and his *L'Allegro* and *Il Penseroso*, but it is very much slighter and more dis-

tant than Dr. Tillyard seems to suppose. For the fact is that the relation between these two poems and Milton's First Prolusion is no more
and no less intimate than that between these poems and several of
Milton's other prolusions, or, for that matter, between these poems
and the whole tradition of academic paradox and debate. Something
of the same kind of wit, something of the same kind of intention,
namely, to show your wit, to show what you could do, is present both
in the poems and in the prolusions. Something, but only something.
For, after the abjurations with which each poems begins, the purely
paradoxical or hyperbolic element in Milton's poems ceases, if it is
present at all, to be felt as paradox or hyperbole. In this respect
L'Allegro and *Il Penseroso* differ greatly, not only from some of the
outrageously and quite unseriously paradoxical poems of Donne, but
even from such a poem as Marvell's *The Garden.*

> No white nor red was ever seen
> So am'rous as this lovely green.

Throughout Marvell's praise of the garden we are delightfully aware
of the element of hyperbole and paradox, whereas Milton's praise of
the /7/ pleasures of mirth and of melancholy is, in comparison, as
unhyperbolical as, let us say, Ben Jonson's Virgilian and Horatian
praise of a country life in his epistle To Sir Robert Wroth.

Each of Milton's poems might almost be described as a Catalogue
of Delights, a formula which relates them, not merely to the two
poems of Fletcher and Strode, but also to Marlowe's *Passionate Shepherd*, Ralegh's reply thereto (both printed in *Englands Helicon*),
and to the many imitations (including Donne's *The Baite*) which
those two poems provoked. Todd, indeed, in his introductory remarks
to *L'Allegro*, says that it has been observed (he does not say by
whom) that the concluding lines of Marlowe's and Ralegh's poems,

> If these delights thy mind may move,
> Then live with me, and be my love,

"seem to have furnished Milton with the hint for the last lines both of
his *Allegro* and *Penseroso*".[2]

II

The subject of the two poems, then, is the contrast between the
pleasures of mirth and the pleasures of melancholy, and they have
some relation, though not, perhaps, a very close one, to a well-

[2]*Poetical Works of John Milton*, 2nd ed., 1809, VI, 69.

established academic and poetic tradition of witty and paradoxical debate. Let us now return to Dr. Johnson's complaint that the contrast between the two poems and the two kinds of pleasure is not great enough, and to the question of what exactly Milton meant by melancholy.

"I know not" Johnson remarked,

whether the characters are kept sufficiently apart. No mirth can, indeed, be found in his melancholy; but I am afraid that I always meet some melancholy in his mirth.

In a sense Johnson was right. He was aware of some apparent inconsistency, and it lies, I think, in a certain disparity between programme and performance, between what we are led to expect and what we actually get: that is to say, the melancholy abjured in the introductory stanza of *L'Allegro* as

<blockquote>loathed Melancholy
Of Cerberus, and blackest midnight born,</blockquote>

/8/ is not the kind of melancholy which is invoked and of which the pleasures are described in *Il Penseroso*; and the heart-easing mirth invoked at the beginning of *L'Allegro*, together with

<blockquote>Jest and youthful Jollity,
Quips and Cranks, and wanton Wiles,</blockquote>

and so forth, has only the very slightest connexion with the mood or moods whose pleasures are actually described in the course of the poem. The mood of *L'Allegro* is not really the mood of Strode's lines against melancholy, although, as I have suggested, it was probably Fletcher's praise of melancholy and Strode's reply to it which suggested to Milton the idea of his two companion poems. Milton's two poems are less antithetical than Fletcher's and Strode's. The mood of Strode's poem,

<blockquote>Returne my joyes and hither bring
A heart not taught to speake but sing,
A jolly spleen, an inward feast,
A causelesse laugh without a jest,</blockquote>

and so forth, is indeed the mood of the opening lines of *L'Allegro*, of the invocation of "heart-easing Mirth" and of "Laughter holding both

his sides"; but although Milton can abstractly approve of such a
mood and abstractly personify it, he is, of course, quite incapable of
evoking, with pleasure to himself and to his readers, a succession of
scenes in all of which he shall appear laughing and holding both
his sides, tripping on light fantastic toe, and otherwise joyfully-
jollificating. Therefore, as soon as the invocation is finished, as soon
as personification gives place to exemplification, as soon as L'Allegro
himself appears and proceeds to go through his round of day-time and
evening pleasures, there is a very considerable sobering down. As
Warton observed:

> There is specifically no mirth in contemplating a fine landscape.
> And even his landscape, although it has flowery meads and flocks,
> wears a shade of pensiveness; and contains *russet* lawns, fallows
> *grey*, and *barren* mountains, overhung with *labouring* clouds. Its
> old turreted mansion peeping from the trees, awakens only a
> train of solemn and romantic, perhaps melancholy, reflection.
> Many a pensive man listens with delight to the milk-maid *singing
> blithe*, to the mower *whetting his scythe*, and to a distant peal of
> village bells. He chose such illustrations as minister matter for
> true poetry and genuine description. Even his most brilliant
> imagery is mellowed with the sober hues of philosophic medi-
> tation.[3] /9/

And just as the exemplifications of cheerfulness in *L'Allegro* are very
different from the personifications of it, so too both the personifications and exemplifications of melancholy in *Il Penseroso* have nothing
in common with the "loathed Melancholy" abjured at the beginning
of *L'Allegro*, and much in common with the rather attractive, romantic, and luxurious melancholy exemplified in Fletcher's poem.
Indeed, one may say that Strode, whose poem does not get beyond
personifying various aspects of cheerfulness, suggested to Milton the
idea of personification, while Fletcher, who exemplifies what he
means by melancholy,

> Fountaine heads, and pathlesse Groves,
> Places which pale passion loves,

suggested to him the idea of exemplifying, as distinct from merely
personifying, the two moods; although, when he actually got to work,
Milton found that he could follow Fletcher more closely than he

---

[3]*Poems upon Several Occasions by John Milton*, 2nd ed., 1791, p. 97.

could follow Strode. He could, that is to say, amplify and diversify and sublimate Fletcher's exemplifications of melancholy, but he could not exemplify, as distinct from merely personifying, the boisterousness of Strode's reply. And exemplification rather than personification was to provide the main substance of his poems, if only because they were to be very much longer than the pair which suggested them.

Nevertheless, although the moods of *L'Allegro* and *Il Penseroso* are less sharply contrasted than in the poems of Fletcher and Strode, although it is only in the rhetorical introductory abjurations and the personification of Mirth and her companions that anything of the originally crude antithesis appears, and although even Warton, a great admirer of these poems, agrees with Johnson in finding some mixture of melancholy in Milton's mirth, there still remains a contrast between the moods of the two poems which is both greater and subtler than has commonly been noticed, if not by readers, at any rate by critics. Perhaps I can best indicate the nature of this contrast by remarking that while L'Allegro's pleasures, though far from boisterous, nearly all have some admixture or suggestion of human society and are of the kind which, in some degree, take one, as the saying is, out of oneself, the pleasures described in *Il Penseroso* are more solitary, more introspective, more purely the pleasures of reverie and of solitary contemplation and imagination. L'Allegro, although he scarcely, perhaps, takes any very active share in them, is still fairly continuously aware of the doings of his fellow-men, and reflections of their activities and pleasures largely determine and largely colour his moods. What would his morning walk be without the sound /10/ of the huntsman's horn, the whistling ploughman, the singing milkmaid, the scythe-whetting mower, and the counting shepherds? Later he approaches the smoking cottage chimney of Thyrsis and Corydon and closes his round of day-time pleasures among country-dancers and story-tellers. His evening pleasures are essentially sociable: tournaments, masques, and comedies. And even when he is alone he looks around him with delighted attention and is taken out of himself by what he sees: nibbling sheep, labouring clouds, daisy-pied meadows, brooks and rivers, romantically embowered towers. The pleasures of Il Penseroso are much more brooding and solitary. Indeed, only once is there any suggestion of human society, when, at the very end of the poem, he hears organ and choir in some cathedral or college chapel. He begins his night (for apparently he does a good part of his sleeping by day) with a stroll in some lonely wood, listening to the nightingale, gazing at the wandering moon, hearing the distant curfew —

sights and sounds more likely to prolong than to interrupt his reverie. He then sits alone by the glowing embers of his hearth and ascends to his lonely tower, where he reads Plato, Greek tragedies (L'Allegro did not read, but visited, comedies) and various romantic poems. When day comes he again repairs to his wood to rest and dream by a brookside, and then, after pacing the studious cloister, first encounters his fellow-beings at divine service.

During the seventeenth century the word melancholy had many different senses and shades of meaning. The noun, in what may be called its strict or proper sense, denoted that dark and dangerous mental disease of melancholia, produced partly by physical causes, such as lack of exercise or ill-regulated diet, and partly by indulgence in certain mental habits, which Burton describes and for which he suggests remedies in his famous book.

> Loathed Melancholy
> Of *Cerberus* and blackest midnight born.

In Shakespeare the word nearly always denotes a disposition which is regarded as unpleasant, unfortunate, or deplorable: Viola's imaginary sister fell into a green and yellow melancholy, and Hamlet feared that the ghost might be a devil which, out of his weakness and his melancholy, was abusing him to damn him. And in Elizabethan usage generally the word denoted, if not the actual disease of melancholia, at any rate a mood of habitual sadness and depression, true though it be that the mood was often affected by persons with pretensions to superior refinement. It was, characteristically, during the more analytic and introspective seven- /11/ teenth century that the word came to be used to denote a certain tender and pensive sadness which, at times perhaps not without some sense of guiltiness and of playing with fire, was regarded as positively agreeable. William Drummond, for example, declared in one of his madrigals that when his mistress wept

> A sweet Melancholie my Senses keepes;[4]

Fletcher declared that

> Nothing's so daintie sweet as lovely melancholy;

while Milton in *Il Penseroso* invokes "divinest Melancholy", and in

---

[4]*Poems*, ed. Kastner, I, 35.

Comus (l. 545) makes the Attendant Spirit describe himself as having been

> Wrapt in a pleasing fit of melancholy.

The history of the adjective is similar. Shakespeare's "melancholy Jaques" is saturnine rather than sweetly pensive; when Capulet, after the discovery of the supposed death of Juliet, declares

> All things that are ordained festival
> Turn from their office to black funeral,

and speaks of "melancholy bells" (IV, v, 86), he means sad, gloomy, dismal bells, and when Orlando in *As You Like It* exclaims to the banished Duke and his company

> But whate'er you are
> That in this desert inaccessible
> Under the shade of melancholy boughs
> Lose and neglect the creeping hours of time,

he means that he finds their situation gloomy and depressing, rather frightening, perhaps a little pathetic: certainly not that he finds it agreeably romantic. Nevertheless, some forty years later (8 October, 1641) Evelyn thus described the royal park at Brussels:

> From hence we walked into the Parke, which for being intirely within the walls of the Citty is particularly remarkable; nor is it less pleasant than if in the most solitary recesses, so naturally is it furnish'd with whatever may render it agreeable, melancholy, and country-like. /12/

In the early part of 1659 Anthony a Wood was taken by a friend to visit one Hannibal Baskervyle who inhabited "a private and lone house in or near Bagley Wood", "an old house situated in a romancey place". This Mr. Baskervyle was very civil, "but A. W. found him to be a melancholy and retir'd man"; nevertheless

> A. Wood afterwards frequented the house, especially in the time of his son Thomas Baskervyle, to refreshe his mind with a melancholy walke, and with the retiredness of the place.[5]

---

[5]*The Life and Times of Anthony a Wood*, ed. Llewelyn Powys, 1932, pp. 64-5.

Thus, while Wood found the melancholy and retiredness of the elder Baskervyle rather depressing, he found the melancholy and retiredness of his grounds, with their "romancey" situation, rather refreshing. And the fact that Wood calls the situation of the place where he took these refreshingly melancholy walks "romancey" suggests that "melancholy" might well have been added to those *Four Words* of which Logan Pearsall Smith so delightfully and illuminatingly investigated the sense-history, and that, accordingly, the origin of romanticism, the romantic mood, and even of the romantic movement might have been taken yet a little further back. For it has often been remarked that something like a new taste had been formed when, shortly after 1650, the words "romancey" and "romantic" began to be commonly applied to scenes which recalled those in old romances, "old castles, mountains and forests, pastoral plains, waste and solitary places."[6] It is true that it is not until the eighteenth century that we hear, from Thomson, of a "fine, romantic kind of melancholy",[7] but already in 1659 we find Wood enjoying a refreshing melancholy in a romancey place, and more than forty years before that Fletcher had discovered the sweetness of melancholy and of scenes where that sweetness could be most luxuriously savoured. It is appropriate that the romantic discovery of the sweetness of melancholy should have been made during the seventeenth century, when so many other important discoveries were made, and when so many characteristically modern movements, including, for all I know, the Romantic Movement, began. Fletcher, perhaps, was the first romantic. Donne was not of the movement, nor, I think, was Jonson, but Milton, the Milton of *Il Penseroso*, certainly was, and, as I shall insist in a moment, it is significant that the Wartons and Hurd and other unimpeachable eighteenth-century romantics, revolting, as school-children say, against the Age of /13/ Prose and Reason, should have continually praised his "romantic" scenes and descriptions.

Before leaving this topic of the kind of melancholy exemplified in *Il Penseroso*, I will notice a conjecture advanced by Thomas Warton in his edition of Milton's Shorter Poems, from which I have already quoted. Neglecting Fletcher and Strode, Warton believed that Milton's two poems had been suggested by a poem of Burton's:

He seems to have borrowed the subject of *L'Allegro* and *Il Penseroso*, together with some particular thoughts, expressions, and

[6]L. Pearsall Smith, *Four Romantic Words*, in *Words and Idioms*, 1928, p. 79.
[7]op. cit., p. 76.

rhymes, more especially the idea of a contrast between these two
dispositions, from a forgotten poem prefixed to the first edition
of Burton's *Anatomie of Melancholy*, entitled "The author's abstract of Melancholy or a Dialogue between Pleasure and Pain".
Here Pain is Melancholy.[8]

Now although it seems to me more than likely that Milton knew both
Burton's poem and Burton's book, and that he took some suggestions
from both, I must insist that Burton's poem is not what Warton says
it is. It is not really a dialogue between Pleasure and Pain, and certainly not a debate between Mirth and Melancholy, but a series of
alternate representations of the pleasures and pains of melancholy in
the serious Burtonian sense: of those oscillations between exaltation
and dejection which attend the unrestrained indulgence of solitary
imagination, and which, if not checked, may finally unhinge the
mind. Here is a representative passage:

> When to my selfe I act and smile,
> With pleasing thoughts the time beguile;
> By a brooke side or wood so greene,
> Vnheard, vnsought for, or vnseene,
> A thousand pleasures doe me blesse,
> And crowne my soule with happinesse.
>   All my ioyes besides are folly,
>   None so sweete as Melancholy.
> When I lie, sit, or walke alone,
> I sigh, I grieue, making great moane,
> In a darke groue, or irkesome denne,
> With discontentes and Furies then,
> A thousand miseries at once,
> Mine heauy heart and soule ensconce.
>   All my griefes to this are iolly,
>   None so soure as Melancholy.[9]

/14/ Burton's poem might, in fact, be regarded as a series of alternate
representations of Fletcher's "sweetest Melancholy" and Milton's
"loathed Melancholy", that melancholy into which, as Burton insists,
sweetest melancholy, if excessively indulged in, may easily turn. For
Burton sweetest melancholy is a dangerous thing, and it is against
such "pleasing melancholy and vaine conceits" that, in his chapter

---

[8] ed. 1791, p. 94.
[9] I quote from the poem as it was first printed, in the third edition, 1628. Warton
wrongly supposed that it had appeared in the first edition, 1621.

"Exercise rectified of Body and Minde", he recommends sight-seeing, recreation and study. I will quote some scattered sentences from the chapter, for it contains, as Warton observed, many parallels with Milton's poems.

> To walke amongst Orchards, Gardens, Bowers, and Arbors, arti-
> ficiall Wildernesses, and greene thickets, Arches, Groues, Pooles,
> Fishponds, betwixt wood and water in a faire Meddowe, by a
> riuer side, to disport in some pleasant plaine, or runne vp a steepe
> hill, or sit in a shady seat, must needs bee a delectable recrea-
> tion . . . To see some Pageant, or sight go by, as at Coronations,
> Weddings, and such like solemnities, to see an Embassadour or a
> Prince met, receaued, entertained with Masks, shews, fire-works,
> &c. . . . The Country hath it's recreations, the Citty it's seuerall
> Gymnicks and exercises, Maygames, Feasts, Wakes, & merry
> meetings to solace themselues . . . *Dancing, Singing, Masking,
> Mumming, Stage-playes,* howsoeuer they be heauily censured by
> some seuere *Catoes,* yet if opportunely and soberly used, may
> iustly be approued . . . To read, walke and see Mappes, Pictures,
> Statues, old Coynes of severall sorts in a fayre Gallery, artificiall
> perspectiue glasses, old reliques, Roman antiquities, variety of
> colors.[10]

Burton is here recommending to the man carried away with "a pleasing melancholy and vaine conceits" various things that will "take him out of himself", make him less introspective and more extravert. And if anyone positively insists on somehow bringing Burton into *L'Allegro* and *Il Penseroso*, I think we might at least allow him to maintain that in *L'Allegro* Milton has exemplified various pleasures and activities (many of them mentioned by Burton) which will correct the pleasing, the sweetest, the divinest melancholy of *Il Penseroso*, and prevent it from turning into Melancholia. Not that Il Penseroso lives entirely in his own solitary imagination; he does, after all, spend a considerable time reading in his lonely tower and he regularly attends divine service. Even when Milton is most characteristically seventeenth century he nearly always is so with a difference. His divinest melancholy is less paradoxical than Fletcher's sweetest melancholy, less illicit, less a kind of secret indulgence. Milton, after all, identifies himself, at least to a considerable extent, with /15/ the two characters, and he just cannot imagine himself as indulging in any mood or pleasure that is at all reprehensible.

---

[10]Part. 2, Sect. 2, Memb. 4, ed. 1621, pp. 341-51.

III

Having now seen more clearly what is the real nature of the contrast between the two poems and what Milton meant by melancholy,
let us proceed to consider *L'Allegro* and *Il Penseroso* as descriptive
poems.

It will be well to apply first the method of comparison and to decide in what sense they are not descriptive, and then to apply the
method of analysis, and, proceeding from the more general to the
more particular, to decide precisely in what sense they are. Let us
begin with Warton's statement that they may be called "the two first
descriptive poems in the English language". What Warton and his
contemporaries meant by a descriptive poem was one where description was not merely incidental or illustrative but essential, a poem
which existed purely for the sake of its descriptions, and whose descriptions were mainly of natural sights and sounds, not of individual
human beings, though sometimes, perhaps, of typical human activities. Milton's poems, it is true, are not purely descriptive in this
sense, since they are controlled by an idea, that of the exemplification of the pleasures appropriate to two contrasted but complemen-
tary moods; nevertheless we may be content without quibbling to
regard them as examples of what is ordinarily meant by descriptive
poetry.

Have they any predecessors? They are obviously different from, on
the one hand, the purely topographical or guide-book description of
Drayton's *Poly-Olbion* and, on the other hand, from the almost purely
witty description of Donne's two verse-letters entitled *The Storme* and
The Calme. The Donne who wrote these two poems may perhaps be
regarded as the originator of a kind of descriptive, or professedly descriptive, poetry which became very popular during the seventeenth
century, and of which the formula would seem to be: to how many
other things, ideas, experiences can this particular experience, or this
particular object in front of me, be related? The chief characteristic
of this kind of poetry is the ingenious simile, and the poet is far less
concerned with his professed subject, which may be almost completely indifferent to him, than with the ingenious things he can
find to say about it, the number of apparently unlikely things and
ideas to which he can somehow succeed /16/ in relating it. Clearly,
L'Allegro and *Il Penseroso* are quite outside this tradition, although
they do contain one or two ingenious similes. So far from being indifferent to what he is describing, Milton is preoccupied with it,
fascinated by it, in love with it. His two poems, then, are descriptive

neither in the topographical manner of Drayton nor in the purely witty manner of Donne. Their only predecessors or prototypes are certain "Catalogues of Delights" (if I may repeat my own phrase) and certain descriptive exemplifications of more or less romantic moods — Fletcher's lines on melancholy, Burton's poem prefixed to the *Anatomy*, some of the descriptions in Beaumont and Fletcher's plays, notably, perhaps, those of and by the wronged Aspasia in *The Maid's Tragedy*.

What, then, of their successors? How do they stand in relation to later poems which may be classified as descriptive? An interesting piece for comparison is that long and rather rambling poem on Appleton House which Marvell wrote sometime in 1651 or 1652, after, I cannot but think, he had bought and read Milton's 1645 volume. For *Appleton House* stands somewhere between the purely witty manner of Donne and Milton's manner in *L'Allegro* and *Il Penseroso*: Marvell is as witty and ingenious as Donne, but, like Milton, he is also in love with what he is describing:

> And now to the Abbyss I pass
> Of that unfathomable Grass,
> Where Men like Grashoppers appear,
> But Grashoppers are Gyants there:
> They, in there squeking Laugh, contemn
> Us as we walk more low then them:
> And, from the Precipices tall
> Of the green spir's, to us do call.

> To see Men through this Meadow Dive,
> We wonder how they rise alive,
> As, under Water, none does know
> Whether he fall through it or go.
> But, as the Marriners that sound,
> And show upon their head the Ground,
> They bring up Flow'rs so to be seen,
> And prove they've at the Bottom been.

Milton is obviously far less witty than Marvell, but, on the other hand, he is far wittier in the seventeenth-century sense than the almost professional nature poets of the eighteenth and nineteenth centuries. *L'Allegro* and *Il Penseroso* are not descriptive poetry in the sense in which /17/ Thomson's *Seasons*, or Wordsworth's *Poems on the Naming of Places*, or many famous things by Tennyson are descriptive poetry. Milton does not set out to give minute descriptions of natural scenes and natural objects, but to give precise descriptions, precise exemplifications, precise evocations of the pleasures appropriate to two contrasted moods. His outlines, the directions he gives to our imagination, are as precise and concise as possible, but he generally leaves us to fill in the visual detail for ourselves.

> Or let my Lamp at midnight hour,
> Be seen in some high lonely Towr —

That example will do as well as any: a *seen* lamp in a tower that is high and lonely. Whether the tower be old and grey, round or square, ruinous, ivy-mantled, moss-grown or lichenous, we may decide for ourselves. This very important distinction between precision of outline, or of imaginative direction, achieved mainly by the use of most carefully chosen adjectives, and minuteness of visual detail, is one that has been completely overlooked by Mr. Eliot in perhaps the most unfortunate of all his writings on Milton[11]: after declaring that, for his purposes, the most important fact about Milton is his blindness, he there complains that "the imagery in *L'Allegro* and *Il Penseroso* is all general", and that, among other things, the whistling ploughman is not individualized. Was Mr. Eliot, I wonder, like Irving Babbitt, recoiling from what seemed to him a symptom of romanticism? For there can, I think, be little doubt that it was the essentially evocative nature of Milton's descriptions which led many of his eighteenth-century admirers to call them romantic. Thomas Warton, for example, in the Preface to his edition, sees in Milton's shorter poems 'fiction and fancy . . . picturesque description and romantic imagery.' Consider, as a description that would probably have seemed to Warton and his contemporaries especially romantic, this from *Il Penseroso:*

> And missing thee, I walk unseen
> On the dry smooth-shaven Green,
> To behold the wandring Moon,
> Riding neer her highest noon,
> Like one that had bin led astray
> Through the Heav'ns wide pathles way;
> And oft, as if her head she bow'd,
> Stooping through a fleecy cloud.

/18/ What, especially the third of those couplets, could be more "romantic"? Shelley might almost have written it, the Shelley of "Art

---

[11]"A Note on the Verse of John Milton" in *Essays and Studies*, XXI (1935).

thou pale for weariness . . . ?" It is true that Shelley dwells on the imagined loneliness of the moon more lingeringly and emphatically than Milton, but the two descriptions, the two ways of seeing it, even the two ways of saying it, still remain strikingly similar. Critics have often complained of a lack of mystery in *Paradise Lost*, but both there and in Milton's shorter poems there is no lack of a suggestiveness that may not inappropriately be called romantic. Milton is commonly regarded, and perhaps rightly, as the most classical of our poets, and yet, as I have observed, we find many eighteenth-century precursors of the so-called Romantic Revival continually praising what seem to them his romantic descriptions, his romantic wildness, his romantic fancy. One could quite plausibly maintain that the classical Milton is the most romantic of seventeenth-century poets. One could also maintain that the official romantics (if I may so describe them) tended to exploit and overemphasize what in Milton remain elements in a balanced whole. The wandering moon and the sound of the far-off curfew,

> Over some wide-water'd shoar,
> Swinging slow with sullen roar,

occupy only a few lines of *Il Penseroso*, whereas with a full-blown romantic each might well occupy a whole poem. We have already noticed some interesting differences and resemblances between *L'Allegro* and *Il Penseroso*, as descriptive poems, and Marvell's *Appleton House*: compare them with those two indisputably beautiful and indisputably romantic poems, Collins's "Ode to Evening" and Keats's "Ode to Autumn". In comparison with Milton, Collins and Keats (I do not say it in any pejorative sense) are much more monotonous, much more willing to linger and luxuriate in single images and single moods. I will leave the subject with a pregnant observation of W. P. Ker's: "Romance is often near its best with authors who are not thinking about it, or who think other things more important."[12]

---

[12]*Collected Essays*, 1925, II, 318.

Maren-Sofie Røstvig

From John Milton*

Milton's *L'Allegro* and *Il Penseroso* represent the finest early flower-
ing of the *beatus ille* tradition in English poetry. Only Andrew
Marvell's 'The Garden' can be said to equal, perhaps to surpass,
Milton's lines on the joys of rural conviviality and of rural solitude.
Both poems present pictures of the joys of life, the chief difference
being that *L'Allegro* depicts the happy man as a rural gentleman-
farmer in the manner of Ben Jonson's Sir Robert Wroth, while
Il Penseroso transforms him into a solitary Serene Contemplator in
the manner of Casimire and Habington. The poems, then, are com-
plementary and not contradictory; each is concerned with a special
human type and with the kind of happy life preferred by each. The
one type is vigorous and extrovert, the other pensive, reflective, and
introvert. Each is placed in a congenial setting and made to pursue
suitable activities. Because their personalities are directly opposed,
they find happiness in settings and activities which are equally
opposed.

Milton's fondness for rural solitude found early expression in one
of his Latin orations written at Cambridge after the Long Vacation
of 1631:

> I myself invoke the glades and streams and beloved elms of the
> farms under which during the summer just gone by . . . I recall
> . . . that I enjoyed the highest favour of the Muses, where amid

---

*Reprinted from *The Happy Man: Studies in the Metamorphoses of a Classical
Ideal.* New York: Humanities Press Inc., 1962 and Oslo: Norwegian Universities
Press, 1962, I, 100-07, by permission.

fields and remote woodlands I have even seemed to myself to
have been able to grow up as it were in seclusion.[1]

Milton would have been thoroughly familiar with the rural passages
found in Horace and Virgil, and an imitation of these would form
a suitable task for a budding poet. *L'Allegro* exploits the realistic
details typical of the rural ode and also the Horatian practice of
pursuing the course of a single day. Thus to begin with we watch
the coming of dawn, and listen to the crowing of the /101/ cock and
to the cheerful sound of hounds and horn. Then we encounter the
ploughman, the milkmaid, the mower, and the shepherd, and we
share their 'sunshine holiday' which lasts until 'daylight fail', and
ale is passed round to the telling of stories. The subsequent passage
on 'towered cities' breaks the *beatus ille* pattern, but it was obviously
needed to off-set the pensive man's preference for complete solitude.

   L'Allegro contains no verbal *beatus ille* echoes, no tell-tale opening
words patterned after Horace, Virgil, or Martial. However, the pattern
of the happy day is traditional enough, and so are the various rural
activities indulged in by the Happy Man and his associates. The rural
and the pastoral are not kept entirely distinct; pastoral characters
like Corydon and Thyrsis occur, but their activities are realistic
enough. The tradition of the realistic pastoral comes quite close to
the rural ode, the form or genre being the chief difference. In form,
L'Allegro adheres to no previously established pattern; the unique
character of Milton's tetrameter couplets has often been commented
on. It seems nevertheless reasonable to associate the form with the
ode in view of the fact that tetrameter couplets were frequently used
in the translation of Horatian odes. . . . /106/

   Both Virgil and Milton supplement their austere pictures of the
quest for truth with appealing descriptions of the peacefulness and
sensuous richness of rural scenes. Thus lines 132-154 of Milton's poem
should be compared with lines 467-471 and 485-489 of the second
Georgic.[2] Both poets prefer the dark shade, the cool glens, the secret

---

[1] *The Works of John Milton* (Columbia University Press, 1936), XII, 249 f. The
quotation is taken from the English translation of the Seventh Prolusion.
[2] To facilitate comparison, I quote the English translation of the relevant lines in
Virgil:
'Yet theirs is repose without care, and a life that knows no fraud, but is rich in
treasures manifold. Yea, the ease of broad domains, caverns, and living lakes, and
cool vales, the lowing of the kine, and soft slumber beneath the trees — all are
theirs. They have woodland glades and the haunts of game . . . let my delight be
the country, and the running streams amid the dells — may I love the waters and
the woods, though fame be lost. O for those plains, and Spercheus, and Taygetus,
where Spartan girls hold Bacchic rites! O for one to set me in the cool glens of
Haemus, and shield me under the branches' mighty shade!' Quoted from the Loeb
edition.

caves, and the soft slumber beneath the trees. The humming of bees, on the other hand, and the sound of the woodman may have been fetched from Virgil's first Eclogue, lines 51-58.[3] Milton retained the bees, but he transformed the song of the woodman and the cooing of the pigeons into sweet music, sent by some unseen genius of the wood, just as he previously had transformed Virgil's reference to the howls of hungry Acheron into 'those *Daemons* that are found / In fire, air, flood, or under ground'. A further classical parallel may be located in Horace's second Epode, lines 23-28.[4] Milton's description of the 'Waters murmuring' which 'Entice the dewy-feathered Sleep' forms a fairly exact echo of Horace's fountains which 'plash with their flowing waters, a sound to invite sound sleep'. The idea, of course, is a poetic commonplace, but to a scholar like Milton an attempt to describe this particular type of scene would surely call up memories of these popular lines by Horace and Virgil. Nor must we undervalue the intellectual satisfaction which this age derived from being able to introduce a classical echo into original compositions. The ability to recognise such echoes, and perhaps perceive what unexpected twist of meaning has been created by the new context, formed part of the pleasure of reading poetry. /107/

To summarise: *L'Allegro* and *Il Penseroso* present *picturae loquentes* of the vivacious, gregarious man whose happiness is unconscious, and of the contemplative or pensive man, whose happiness derives from that clear light which shines in his own breast. Both are songs of joy—the first of the joys of a convivial existence, the second of the more sublime joys of solitude. Both are connected with the classical tradition of the *beatus vir*, but the neo-Stoic bias of the second is the result of a completely contemporary interpretation of the idea of human happiness. We have traced the gradual development of this interpretation through the original *beatus ille* poetry of the early seventeenth century, and also through those prose character sketches which present human virtues and vices in neo-Stoic terms. Milton's companion poems therefore represent the culmination of a trend typical of the early seventeenth century and should be viewed as a contribution to an existing poetic tradition.

---

[3]'Happy old man! Here, amid familiar streams and sacred springs, you shall court the cooling shade ... the hedge whose willow blossoms are sipped by Hybla's bees shall often with its gentle hum soothe you to slumber ... under the towering rock, the woodman's song shall fill the air; while still the cooing woodpigeons, your pets, and the turtle-dove shall cease not their moaning from the skyey elm.'

[4]'Tis pleasant, now to lie beneath some ancient ilex-tree, now on the matted turf. Meanwhile the rills glide between their high banks; birds warble in the woods; the fountains plash with their flowing waters, a sound to invite soft slumbers.'

T. S. Eliot

From A Note on the Verse of John Milton*

/33/The most important fact about Milton, for my purposes, is his blindness. I do not mean that to go blind in middle life is itself enough to determine the whole nature of a man's poetry. Blindness must be considered in conjunction with Milton's personality and character, and the peculiar education which he received. It must also be considered in connexion with his devotion to, and expertness in, the art of music. Had Milton been a man of very keen senses—I mean of *all* the five senses—his blindness would not have mattered so much. But for a man whose sensuousness, such as it was, had been withered early by book-learning, and whose gifts were naturally aural, it mattered a great deal. It would seem, indeed, to have helped him to concentrate on what he could do best.

At no period is the visual imagination conspicuous in Milton's poetry. It would be as well to give a few illustrations of what I mean by visual imagination. From *Macbeth*:

> This guest of summer,
> The temple-haunting martlet, does approve
> By his loved mansionry that the heaven's breath
> Smells wooingly here: no jutty, frieze,
> Buttress, nor coign of vantage, but this bird /34/
> Hath made his pendant bed and procreant cradle:
> Where they most breed and haunt, I have observed
> The air is delicate.

*Reprinted from *Essays and Studies by Members of the English Association*, XXI (1936), 32-40, by permission of the Clarendon Press, Faber and Faber Ltd., and the executrix of the author's estate. Only pp. 33-35 are reprinted here.

It may be observed that such an image, as well as another familiar quotation from a little later in the same play,

> Light thickens, and the crow
> Makes wing to the rooky wood

not only offer something to the eye, but, so to speak, to the common sense. I mean that they convey the feeling of being in a particular place at a particular time. The comparison with Shakespeare offers another indication of the peculiarity of Milton. With Shakespeare, far more than with any other poet in English, the combinations of words offer perpetual novelty; they enlarge the meaning of the individual words joined: thus 'procreant cradle', 'rooky wood'. In comparison, Milton's images do not give this sense of particularity, nor are the separate words developed in significance. His language is, if one may use the term without disparagement, *artificial* and *conventional*.

> O'er the smooth *enamelled* green ...
> ... paths of this drear wood
> The nodding horror of whose shady brows
> Threats the forlorn and wandering passenger.

('Shady brow' here is a diminution of the value of the two words from their use in the line from *Dr. Faustus*

> Shadowing more beauty in their airy brows.)

The imagery in *L'Allegro* and *Il Penseroso* is all general:

> While the ploughman near at hand,
> Whistles o'er the furrowed land,
> And the milkmaid singeth blithe,
> And the mower whets his scythe,
> And every shepherd tells his tale
> Under the hawthorn in the dale.

It is not a particular ploughman, milkmaid, and shepherd that Milton sees (as Wordsworth might see them); the sensuous effect of these verses is entirely on the ear, and is joined to the concepts of ploughman, milkmaid, and shepherd. /35/ Even in his most mature work, Milton does not infuse new life into the word, as Shakespeare does.

> The sun to me is dark
> And silent as the moon,

> When she deserts the night
> Hid in her vacant interlunar cave.

Here *interlunar* is certainly a stroke of genius, but is merely combined with 'vacant' and 'cave', rather than giving and receiving life from them. Thus it is not so unfair, as it might at first appear, to say that Milton writes English like a dead language.

Phyllis MacKenzie

From Milton's Visual Imagination: An Answer to T. S. Eliot*

Probably no major English poetry is further removed in point of technique from twentieth-century poetry than is John Milton's. It is not surprising, therefore, that Milton should be attacked by many modern poets and critics who convince themselves that he has not written great poetry because he has not written in the way that they would have him write. Thus, in his "Note on the Verse of John Milton,"[1] Mr. T. S. Eliot declares, "At no period is the visual imagination conspicuous in Milton's poetry," or again, "Milton may be said never to have seen anything"—simply because Milton's descriptive technique, like his whole poetic design, is different from Eliot's own and from that of the poets he most admires.

That such is the case is obvious from the two chief objections which Mr. Eliot raises to Milton's descriptions. First, he complains that Milton's imagery is general, unlike Shakespeare's, for instance, which "conveys the feeling of being at a particular place at a particular time." Secondly, he believes that Milton, again unlike Shakespeare, combines words in descriptive passages, but does not marry them; that is, according to Mr. Eliot, in combination each of Milton's words stands aloof, not giving and receiving larger life from the others.

I wish to begin my defence of Milton's visual imagination at the spearhead of Mr. Eliot's attack—his comparison of passages from Shakespeare's *Macbeth* with various passages from Milton. The comparison is valuable in itself as a kind of process of condensation by

*Reprinted from *University of Toronto Quarterly*, XVI (October, 1946), 17-29, by permission of University of Toronto Press and the author.
[1]See *Essays and Studies by Members of the English Association*, XXI, collected by Herbert Read.

which the most distinctive aspects of Milton's visual imagination may
be precipitated. Mr. Eliot's conclusions from the comparison, however,
are vitiated by two false assumptions. First of all, he takes it for
granted that short passages of Miltonic description may be quoted in
isolation as adequate illustrations of the whole technique. In reality,
it is difficult to study Milton's descriptive technique except in large
units, for the smaller units become completely active only when read
in the cumulative sequence of the whole. Secondly, Mr. Eliot's deduc-
tions from the comparison are made on the assumption that Milton
was attempting to achieve the same effects in his descriptions as
Shakespeare in his. Actually, of course, a comparison of the two
descriptive techniques has significance only when studied in close
relation to the divergent purposes of the poet and the playwright.
Aiming at the cumulative expression of a vast, interactive design in
his major works, Milton was consciously guarding against abortive or
disruptive particularization in description. His purpose was not to
create a series of /18/ self-contained pictures, each assertively memorable in itself. Rather, he aimed at a progressive and composite
visualization, in which all details should spring to ordered life within
the continuously evolving pattern of the whole.

Before beginning a more specific examination of Milton's distinctive
aims and techniques in description, it may be well to look at an
example of particularized description. Mr. Eliot, quite rightly, holds
that Milton's imagery is, on the whole, general. However, it is significant that when the poet saw fit momentarily to arrest the movement
of the reader's mind in a specific, vividly sensuous picture, he was
quite capable of doing so; take, for instance, the following lines from
Comus:

> millions of spinning Worms,
> That in their green shops weave the smooth-haired silk.[2]

It would be difficult to find a more perfect example of the kind of
Shakespearean description which, through the careful selection and
compression of particularized detail, "conveys the feeling of being
at a particular place at a particular time." That such was not Milton's
usual method does not indicate any failure of his visual imagination,
as Mr. Eliot would have us believe. It is the result rather of the most

---

[2]*Comus*, 715-16. It is significant that Mr. Leavis, one of the most violent detractors
of Milton, praises the whole "bounty speech," from which these lines were taken, in
New Bearings in Poetry.

perfect adaptation of his descriptive technique to his total artistic purpose.

Mr. Eliot's comparison of a speech of Banquo's with a short passage from "L'Allegro" provides a good starting place for a discussion of the typically Miltonic descriptive technique. The two selections, quoted below, are used by Mr. Eliot as evidence in support of his chief objection—that Milton's imagery is predominantly general.

> This guest of summer,
> The temple-haunting martlet, does approve
> By his loved mansionry that the heaven's breath
> Smells wooingly here; no jutty, frieze,
> Buttress, nor coign of vantage, but this bird
> Hath made his pendent bed and procreant cradle;
> Where they most breed and haunt, I have observed
> The air is delicate.[3]

> While the Plowman near at hand,
> Whistles o'er the Furrowed Land,
> And the Milkmaid singeth blithe,
> And the Mower whets his scythe,
> And every Shepherd tells his tale
> Under the Hawthorn in the dale.[4]

/19/ To begin with, of course, the justice of Mr. Eliot's observation must be admitted. The passage from "L'Allegro," with its generalized detail, fails to transmit the sense of immediate and specific reality which is conveyed by Banquo's speech. The difference, however, does not arise from any deficiency in Milton of the capacity to visualize concretely. Instead it is the result of the very different artistic purposes which the two quoted passages were meant to fulfill. Shakespeare, in Banquo's speech, was intent upon conjuring up a complete realistic setting for his action, by means of the careful manipulation of a few specific details. The emotional atmosphere of the speech is, therefore, derivative, not primary, extracted directly from the observed concrete detail. Milton, on the contrary, was not, in "L'Allegro," approaching nature directly; he was not seeking the "inscape" of the particular, not intent upon springing open the pod of the concrete detail and fostering the natural growth of the seed within. He began with a preconceived pattern, the pattern of a mood, and from nature recreated details to fit that pattern. In order, therefore, to subordinate the visual

---

[3]*Macbeth*, 1.6.
[4]"L'Allegro," 63-8.

details to his total design, to limit the concrete visualization to the purposes of the poem, Milton has used, on the whole, generalized epithets.

In a classical poem such as "L'Allegro" we should regard the natural details as a Platonist looks at the parts of the universe. They are the multiple bodyings-forth of an Idea in the mind of the poet. Part of the pleasure for the reader, therefore, is derived from the excitement of watching visual details spring to life, luxuriant and apparently real, which, none the less, bend and taper into the emergent design of the evolving whole. The Plowman, Milkmaid, Mower, and Shepherd of the passage quoted, along with the Cock, the Lark, and even the "labouring clouds" of the poem, are like dancers in a dance. Each is characterized by stylized movements, executed against a stylized background; and both movement and background are keyed to the rhythm of the central mood.

All the steps in the dance, however, are not as formalized as those of the Plowman-Milkmaid group in the passage quoted. Frequently Milton thrusts through to the kernel of a more particular and immediate impression of the real, by means of a piercing word, twisted into a partial metaphor, for instance,

> To hear the Lark begin his flight,
> And singing *startle* the dull night.[5]

or by the more robust realism of the semi-comic picture of the "drudging Goblin," who

> stretch'd out all the Chimney's length,
> Basks at the fire his hairy strength.[6]

In these passages it would almost seem that the Lark and the Goblin were about to step out of the dance and continue existence in a real English /20/ countryside. But they do not step out, and the dance continues uninterrupted. Milton has simply demonstrated the resilience of his pattern by straining it as far as it will go.

The world of "L'Allegro" is the world of the poem, and in that world all details are completely, but never disruptively visualized; for Milton, unlike Mr. Eliot in his own work antecedent to the

---

[5]*Ibid.*, 41-2.
[6]*Ibid.*, 111-12.

Quartets, was not trying "to get beyond poetry."[7] He was not seeking
through the descriptions in "L'Allegro" to burst joy's grape against
the reader's palate, to evoke in him a mood so fiercely sweet, so
all-possessing, that it would draw him irresistibly away from the poem
itself. Milton's description is profoundly evocative, but the emotion it
evokes is ordered and controlled, regulated by the movement of the
poem as a whole and inseparable from the total poetic experience. . . .

---

[7] Using Mr. Eliot's phrase out of context, I am admittedly warping its meaning; but
even warped it will serve to measure the distance between Milton's aim in description
and that of the moderns who attack him.

E. M. W. Tillyard

From *L'Allegro* and *Il Penseroso**

Scholars have not been backward in seeking the literary origins of *L'Allegro* and *Il Penseroso*. Apart from many minor references there are passages that clearly imitate or recall unconsciously poems of Burton, Beaumont and Fletcher, Breton, and Marston. Of these only Burton's poem—*The Author's Abstract of Melancholy* prefixed to the *Anatomy*—has any general bearing. This poem is a dialogue between the pleasing kind and the unpleasing kind of melancholy in the author's brain, and, though this contrast evolves with but small resemblance to Milton's, it is sufficient to have suggested the plan of Milton's poems. But the analogy tells us very little: nothing about the nature of /15/ Milton's poems and nothing about their date. There is, however, another analogy, hitherto undetected, which tells us a great deal more. To put it briefly *L'Allegro* and *Il Penseroso* grew out of Milton's *First Academic Exercise* or *Prolusion*.

Milton's *Prolusions* are exercises in Latin, written from time to time while he was at Cambridge, to fulfil the requirements for getting his degrees. Such exercises were the equivalent—inherited from the Middle Ages—of the modern examination. They were not mere essays, but pleadings in a public debate. The disputant had to be ready to compose his speech in support of either side of the subject at issue, as ordered. Thus in his *Seventh Prolusion*, on the merits of Learning and Ignorance, Milton mentions that he first intended to champion Ignorance but had been requested to change sides. Anyhow, the academic disputation meant a contrast, whether of eulogies or of an attack and a defence.

---

*Reprinted from E. M. W. Tillyard, *The Miltonic Setting*. London: Cambridge University Press, 1938, pp. 1-28, by permission. Only pp. 14-28 are reprinted here.

The *First Prolusion* cannot come later than July 1628, because in it Milton refers to the hostility of the undergraduates to him, which had disappeared by the time he delivered the *Vacation Exercise* or *Sixth Prolusion* at that date. It therefore comes well before any date the critics have assigned to *L'Allegro* and *Il Penseroso*. Concerned with the subject *Whether Day or Night is the more excellent*, it advocates the superior excellence of day. It begins with an elaborate inquiry into the mythical genealogy of Night and Day; goes on to describe the dawning of day and the glory of the sun; and ends by praising day and abusing night. Milton /16/ elaborated the mythology in order to display, as it was his business to do, the extent of his classical learning, and to indulge a rather artless and engaging form of burlesque humour. *L'Allegro* and *Il Penseroso* both begin with mythical genealogies, of Mirth and Melancholy respectively, with less elaboration than the *Prolusion* but (in view of other resemblances) in undoubted imitation of it. The mythology finished, *L'Allegro*, like the *Prolusion*, goes on to describe the day-break, and in such similar terms as to leave no doubt that here the *Prolusion* is its original. Here is the prose account:

Even the birds cannot hide their delight, but leave their nests at peep of dawn and noise it abroad from the tree-tops in sweetest song, or darting upwards as near as they may to the Sun, take their flight to welcome the returning day. First of all these the wakeful cock acclaims the sun's coming, and like a herald bids mankind shake off the bonds of sleep and rise and run with joy to greet the new-born day. The kids skip in the meadows, and beasts of every kind leap and gambol in delight. The sad heliotrope, who all night long has gazed toward the east, awaiting her beloved Sun, now smiles and beams at her lover's approach. The marigold too and rose, to add their share to the joy of all, open their petals and shed abroad their perfume, which they have kept for the Sun alone, and would not give to Night, shutting themselves up within their little leaves at fall of evening. And all the other flowers raise their heads, drooping and weighed down with dew, and offer themselves to the Sun, mutely begging him to kiss away the tear-drops which his absence brought. The Earth too decks herself in lovelier robes to honour the Sun's coming, and the clouds, arrayed in garb of every hue, attend the rising god in festive train and long procession. /17/

In *L'Allegro* the lark who sings 'from his watch tower in the Skies' corresponds to the birds in the passage quoted which 'dart upwards

as near as they may to the Sun'. And in both the cock is mentioned
immediately after the birds. The Cheerful Man,[1] in the poem, comes
to the window and bids good morrow to the dawn; in the prose, mankind is bidden to 'shake off the bonds of sleep, and rise and run to
greet the new-born day'. Closest of all are the descriptions of the
clouds attending the rising sun: compare the last words of the prose
passage with

> Wher the great Sun begins his state,
> Rob'd in flames, and Amber light,
> The clouds in thousand Liveries dight.

Later in the *Prolusion* Milton pictures the world's predicament if
bereft of day and says:

> In vain would the earth bring forth in abundance vines twining
> in many a winding trail, in vain nobly towering trees.

It may be that

> Through the Sweet-Briar, or the Vine,
> Or the twisted Eglantine,

and

> Boosom'd high in tufted Trees,

echo this.

There remains one important detail of resemblance. The first lines
of *L'Allegro*, already quoted and found /18/ so puzzling, are derived
from one or two passages in the *First Prolusion*. Here are the most
relevant:

> Day is the eldest daughter of Heaven, or rather of his Son, be-
> gotten by him, it is said, to be the comfort of the race of men and
> the terror of the infernal god, for fear lest Night should rule un-
> opposed, lest Ghosts and Furies and all that loathsome brood of
> monsters, unchecked by any barrier between Earth and Hades,
> should leave the pit of Hell and make their way even to the upper
> world, and lest wretched Man, enveloped and surrounded by
> murky darkness, should suffer even in this life the tortures of the
> damned.

---

[1] If he, and not the lark, is the subject of *com* in line 45 of *L'Allegro*. The corre-
sponding passage in the *Prolusion* might help to settle the question.

None will you meet save ghosts and spectres, and fearsome goblins who follow in Night's train from the realms below; it is their boast that all night long they rule the earth and share it with mankind. To this end, I think, night sharpens our hearing, that our ears may catch the sooner and our hearts perceive with greater dread the groans of spectres, the screeching of owls and night-birds, and the roaring of lions that prowl in search of prey.

And a little lower down Milton speaks of 'Cimmerian darkness'. The resemblance of these passages to the opening of *L'Allegro* is too strong to need proving in detail; Milton must have had them in mind when he began the poem. Now in their context they are plainly burlesque, especially the second; and it can hardly be doubted that the opening of *L'Allegro* is burlesque also. If so, what was he burlesquing? Immediately, himself. In 1626, when he was seventeen, Milton wrote an ambitious little poem in Latin hexameters on the Gunpowder Plot. He must have concluded that he was trying too much, because he brought it to an abrupt close without recounting the main part of the story in any detail at all. It shows power, but it is /19/ crude and bombastic. Milton must very soon have learnt to see its defects. Here is the passage which he may have been parodying in *L'Allegro* and which is certainly behind parts of the *First Prolusion*:

> Est locus aeternâ septus caligine noctis
> Vasta ruinosi quondam fundamina tecti,
> Nunc torvi spelunca Phoni, Prodotaeque bilinguis
> Effera quos uno peperit Discordia partu.
> Hic inter caementa jacent semifractaque saxa,
> Ossa inhumata virûm, et trajecta cadavera ferro;
> His Dolus intortis semper sedet ater ocellis,
> Jurgiaque, et stimulis armata Calumnia fauces,
> Et Furor, atque viae moriendi mille videntur,
> Et Timor, exanguisque locum circumvolat Horror,
> Perpetuoque leves per muta silentia Manes
> Exululant, tellus et sanguine conscia stagnat.[2]

Behind all three places in Milton there is of course a complex of 'horrid' writing, which need not be discussed—Virgil, Seneca, the Uni-

---

[2]'There is a place hedged in by the eternal gloom of night, once the vast foundation of a ruined abode, now the cave of fierce Murder and double-tongued Treason, whom savage Discord bore at one birth. Here among quarry-stones and broken rocks lie the unburied bones of men and bodies pierced with steel. Here sits dark Fraud for ever with distorted eyes, and Strife, and Calumny, her jaws armed with spikes, and Rage. Here are seen a thousand ways of death. And Fear and pale Horror flit round the place; and continually the insubstantial ghosts howl through the dumb silence, and the earth in sympathy drips with blood.'

versity Wits, Giles and Phineas Fletcher—and he may be glancing at
the whole mode as well as at his immature self. The question *why*
Milton should have opened *L'Allegro* with burlesque will have to wait
till a much more important likeness between the pair of poems and
the *First Prolusion* has been propounded. /20/

Now an academic disputant had to be ready to support either side
of a question set for debate. It is highly probable that Milton had
considered what was to be said in favour of night as well as writing
his speech in favour of day; that he had the idea of the contrasted
eulogy in his mind. Johnson objected to Milton's Cheerful Man and
Meditative Man because they were too much alike; and it is perfectly
true that they do not supply much contrast to their poems. Nevertheless, the poems *are* sharply contrasted, and the contrast is that between day and night. *L'Allegro* written in praise of day corresponds
to the *First Prolusion*; *Il Penseroso* written in praise of night corresponds to what Milton would have said had he been called on to take
the other side. The contrast can be worked out in the most precise
detail. Melancholy, in *L'Allegro*, is at the opening connected with
blackest midnight; Mirth is the daughter of the dawn. Both poems
move in a simple progression of time. In *L'Allegro* the progression
begins with dawn. The lark startles the *dull* night, and the cock routs
retreating night like the stragglers of a defeated army, he 'scatters the
rear of darkness thin'. Homage is paid to the source of daylight—'the
great Sun begins his state'. The action progresses through the day till
in the evening the Cheerful Man carries his cheerfulness into the
hostile realms of night by entering the festivities of the town. Hymen
carries her taper, and mask and pageantry suggest the light of many
candles. *Il Penseroso* is constructed on the same lines, with night and
darkness substituted for day and light. The sun is futile, serving
merely to show the /21/ foolish motes that hover in its beams. Melancholy is dressed in sober black. The progression of time begins with
the evening and the nightingale's song. It is to the credit of the
embers indoors that they give little light: they counterfeit a gloom.
The Meditative Man watches all night and invokes the night ('thus
night oft see me in thy pale career') ; and when day comes he carries
his midnight meditations into the hostile realms of day. Day dawns
chastened, hidden in a cloud. 'And when the sun begins to fling his
flaring beams' the Meditative Man prolongs night into day by seeking
'twilight groves'. Day is hostile, and he seeks to hide himself from
'Day's garish eie" either by sleep or by taking refuge in the 'dimm
religious light' of a cathedral. In fact from first to last the poems are
constructed on the contrasted eulogy of day and night.

I hope the case for deriving *L'Allegro* and *Il Penseroso* from the *First Prolusion* has been made convincing. Here is the last piece of evidence. When Milton wrote the *First Prolusion* he had already connected its subject with poetry, for he says:

> The question whether Day or Night is preferable is no common theme of discussion, and it is now my duty, the task meted out to me this morning, to probe the subject thoroughly and radically, though it might seem better suited to a poetical exercise than to a contest of rhetoric.

L'Allegro and *Il Penseroso* are the 'poetical exercise' on this theme. /22/

4

If Milton derived the idea of *L'Allegro* and *Il Penseroso* from an oration addressed to a university audience, it is probable that he had a similar audience in mind when he composed the poems. Does such an assumption either explain any of their difficulties, or conspicuously fit any of their characteristics?

One difficulty was the bombast with which *L'Allegro* begins. As it stands, with no background, it is meaningless. There is nothing else like it within the poem to check any conjecture as to its character. It is not organic; and to explain it, extrinsic data are necessary. But an academic audience would not have found it obscure; it would have seen the humour as readily as the Classical Sixth at a Public School would fall to a burlesque of Greek tragedy. Every undergraduate would know Ovid with his endless mythology and would be perfectly familiar with the notion of burlesquing it—even without having read *A Midsummer Night's Dream*. Directly they heard of Melancholy being born of Cerberus and blackest Midnight—infamous coupling— they would have a comfortable sense of familiarity and recognition, and begin to grin. Not only would an academic audience be specially quick to detect the burlesque,; it would feel more keenly the force of the opening in the context of the poem. Milton's object is to build up an opening which both in theme and rhythm shall contrast as strikingly as possible with the joy and swing of

> But come thou goddess fair and free,

/23/ breaking in so suddenly. All readers of course appreciate the contrast—indeed they have found the mere clash of differences so delightful that they have omitted to look closely at one of the colliding bodies. The contrast has been considered merely one of gloom and lethargy with light and movement. But an academic audience would have got more of a shock; it must have had its breath fairly taken away by the sudden swing from the familiar, deliberately dismal melodrama to a joyous and serious beauty. Indeed, I have a slight suspicion of a 'stunt', a suspicion confirmed by Milton's having treated his college audience to things not so very different before. In his *Prolusions* he is very fond of alternating the sublime and the ridiculous, and sometimes does so with a good deal of charm. The most impressive example is when, in the *Sixth Prolusion*, he follows his comic speech with the sublime rhetoric of his *Lines at a Vacation Exercise*. But if a 'stunt', how admirably calculated to delight and impress an undergraduate audience! Indeed, it is only in relation to such an audience that the passage under discussion can be either understood or justified. How it can be understood has been discussed: as the high spirits of a young man it can perhaps be justified.

The social tone of the poems is far more appropriate to Cambridge than to Horton. Milton's last years at college were, with the possible exception of his Italian visit, the period of his early life when such a tone is most to be expected. At first he had not been popular and had thought poorly of his fellows, but by the time of the *Sixth Prolusion*, July 1628, the situation had /24/ changed. He says that the old hostility towards him has just changed to friendship and generosity. Moreover, he could not have been invited to take the chief part in so important an affair as this Vacation Exercise had not his talents been appreciated. It is plain that he responded very warmly to the change of opinion and that he was conscious of the social obligations that resulted from it. It is pretty certain that from the summer of 1628 till he took his M.A. in 1632 he was an important person at the University, and that he enjoyed being one. The confidence bred of an appreciative audience and the desire to requite appreciation by considering that audience's likes and dislikes seem to me to be the precise accompaniment to which the airs of *L'Allegro* and *Il Penseroso* are set. And the end of *Il Penseroso*, the prayer for the 'peaceful hermitage' in 'weary age', how charmingly callow, how perfectly appropriate to an audience of boys (one must not forget how young they went to college in those days)! It fits far less well the lips of a man who has retired into studious quiet already. The assumption then that Milton had an academic audience in mind when he wrote *L'Allegro* and *Il Penseroso* seems to me completely justified.

The absence of the poems from the Trinity Manuscript brings with it the question of date. It is in itself but a small piece of evidence in favour of Cambridge rather than Horton: fortified by the discovery that the poems are derived from a university exercise and that they fit a university audience, it becomes a powerful indication that Milton wrote them while still at /25/ college. I think it is legitimate to make a close guess at their date. In style they belong to what I have called elsewhere the poems of Milton's early maturity: those less ambitious poems, beginning with the *Song on May Morning*, written after the ambitious failure of *The Passion*. *The Passion* dates probably in Lent 1630. Milton left Cambridge in the summer of 1632. Some date between these two must be sought. In April 1631 the Marchioness of Winchester died, and Milton celebrated her death in octosyllabics. It is highly probable that he continued his essay in that metre with *L'Allegro* and *Il Penseroso*. They are less indebted to contemporary literature than the *Epitaph*, which suggests Jonson and Browne. But Milton had already shown originality in the *Nativity Ode*; there was nothing to prevent a swift maturing after his initial experiment. The *Seventh Prolusion*, already quoted to prove what dominated Milton's mind at Horton, was almost certainly written in his last year at Cambridge. In it he speaks of the studious retirement which had been interrupted, and in the following passage probably refers to a country holiday in the Long Vacation of 1631:

> I can myself call to witness the woods and rivers and the beloved village elms, under whose shade I enjoyed such sweet intercourse with the Muses, as I still remember with delight. There I too, amid rural scenes and woodland solitudes, felt that I had enjoyed a season of growth in a life of seclusion.

It is very likely that *L'Allegro* and *Il Penseroso* reflect these woods and rivers and trees and that they are the /26/ fruit of that happy season of growth. In brief, they belong to the summer of 1631.

Most readers of Milton will find the above conclusion extremely distasteful; I certainly did myself. To dissociate things so closely and so long linked as *L'Allegro* and Horton is unpleasant, but, the break once made, it should be possible to appreciate the poem more justly, and, by the removal of an impediment, to understand better what Milton was doing at Horton.

A last observation on Milton's addressing his poems to a university audience. That audience mattered much more to him as a poet than has even been supposed. We shall have to accustom ourselves to associating his poems from *Elegia Prima* (1626) to *L'Allegro* and *Il Penseroso* (1631), his *Prolusions*, and his university audience very closely one with another. Such early Latin poems as the elegies on the Esquire Bedell, the Bishop of Ely, and the Vice-Chancellor are obvious instances of such an association. Had he not been ambitious of impressing his fellows as a poet, Milton would never have inserted his *Lines at a Vacation Exercise* in the comic entertainment he was chosen to give before the entire University. The *Second Prolusion*, on the music of the spheres, imitates or is imitated by a passage in the *Nativity Ode*. The lines *Naturam non pati Senium* were written for one of the dons for public recitation. I have no doubt that any one who troubled to compare the *Prolusions* with Milton's contemporary poems in detail would find many unnoticed connections. I fancy that the request to write *Lycidas* sent to /27/ Milton from Cambridge five years after he went down was due, not to *Arcades* and *Comus*, but to his high reputation as a writer of elegies and other occasional verse while at college. Milton's 'fit audience though few' was a *pis aller*: he wanted as wide a fame as he could get; and at college he seems to have succeeded pretty well. Only, he would never compromise his integrity at any price; fame was never allowed to come first. Milton succeeded in being ambitious without the corruption that often infects ambition.

Postscript. In his important study of the chronology of Milton's early poems (*Review of English Studies*, 1935, pp. 1-8), Mr. W. R. Parker confirms the notion that *L'Allegro* and *Il Penseroso* were written in 1631. But see also Professor Merritt Y. Hughes's interesting discussion in his recent edition of Milton (Doubleday, Doran, 1937). Professor Hughes puts 1631 as a tentative date but rightly insists that we cannot say anything more certain than that the poems were written in the later part of Milton's university career. Professor Hughes adds several analogies, including one between the description of the morning in *L'Allegro* and the Latin verses in the Commonplace Book on getting up early and enjoying nature. I should like to correct a false impression my treatment of *Il Penseroso* gave Professor Hughes. He took it that I regarded the whole of *Il Penseroso* as pervaded by an element of irony intended to appeal to the academic audience. But I did not mean that because Milton was aware of his audience, he did not please himself at the same time. /28/ He deals with the kind of things his audience will understand, but he loses himself with all seriousness and without irony in his theme. The youthful touch of the 'peaceful hermitage' in 'weary age' may indeed be, as Professor Hughes says it risks being, a little sentimental, but if so, Milton's youth may excuse a fault not found elsewhere in the poem.

Edward S. LeComte

From From Poem to Poem

E. M. W. Tillyard, on the basis of some resemblance between
the First Prolusion, "Utrum Dies an Nox praestantior sit?", and
"L'Allegro" and "Il Penseroso," has argued that the pair of lyrics
belong to Milton's Cambridge period, instead of his Horton period,
where they are usually placed.[1] In view of the general and detailed
affinities between *Comus* and *Paradise Lost*, such a method of dating
Milton's poetry may now be seen as the specious thing it is. There is
no span of years within his productive lifetime across which Milton
will not and does not reach to borrow from himself. One could argue
as well, probably better, that "L'Allegro" and "Il Penseroso" were
written in the Horton period, because of the phrases connecting them
with *Comus*. One would cite the following:

> Come, and trip it, as you go
> On the light fantastic toe.   ("L'Allegro," 33)

> Come, knit hands, and beat the ground
> In a light fantastic round.   (*Comus*, 143)

/61/ And young and old come forth to play
> On a sunshine holiday.   ("L'Allegro," 97)

> Back, shepherds, back! Enough your play,
> Till next sunshine holiday.   (*Comus*, 958)

---

*Reprinted from *Yet Once More: Verbal and Psychological Pattern in Milton*.
New York: Liberal Arts Press, 1953, pp. 48-68; reprinted New York: AMS Press,
Inc., 1969 by permission. Only pp. 60-61 are reprinted here.
    [1]*The Miltonic Setting* (London 1938), pp. 1-28. See the objection to this method of
dating by A. S. P. Woodhouse, "Notes on Milton's Early Development," *University
of Toronto Quarterly*, XIII (1943), 85 ff.

Married to immortal verse.   ("L'Allegro," 137)

Storied of old in high immortal verse.   (*Comus*, 516)

moon . . . Stooping through a fleecy cloud.
("Il Penseroso," 72)

moon . . . Stoop thy pale visage through an amber cloud.
(*Comus*, 333)

Here is specific resemblance, in the same language, in the same words, even in the same meter and rhyme, in contrast to the elusive analogies on which Tillyard tries to rest his case. But the point is that neither argument deserves credence. Milton is perfectly capable of inserting, as far as blank verse permits, a bit of "L'Allegro" suddenly into *Paradise Lost*:

> fairy elves,
> Whose midnight revels, by a forest side
> Or fountain, some belated peasant sees.   (i, 781)

Actually, "Midnight shout and revelry" is from *Comus* (103), that part of *Comus* which is in the meter of "L'Allegro." Everything is in flux, for we are reckoning with the conscious and the unconscious processes of creation, whose laws have yet to be found. Things we know so well in *Paradise Lost* as "the eastern gate" (iv, 542; xi, 190; xii, 638) and "Elysian flowers" (iii, 359) were already in "L'Allegro" (59; 147). The latter enter in connection with setting Orpheus in paradise, where Milton was to go. Mirth was given "honour due" ("L'Allegro," 37) long before Uriel (iii, 738) and Jesus Christ (v, 817).

Cleanth Brooks

The Light Symbolism in
"L'Allegro-Il Penseroso"*

The most amusing and at the same time probably the most pene-
trating comment on "L'Allegro-Il Penseroso" has to be credited to
Dr. Samuel Johnson. True, Johnson sometimes seems brutally obvious as when he points out that "the gaiety [of L'Allegro does not
spring] from the pleasures of the bottle." We scarcely need to be
warned against attempting to visualize Milton's demure and academic
Platonist tippling his way through the morning landscape. Some of
Johnson's other comments seem quite as pointless without having the
merit of seeming amusing. For example, Johnson tells us that "the
pensive man never loses himself in crowds." To be sure, he does not;
and if he does not, what of it? Yet it has remained for Dr. Johnson
to point out the essential character of the speaker in the two poems,
and several of the pertinent passages are worth quoting:

> Both Mirth and Melancholy are solitary, silent inhabitants of the
> breast, that neither receive nor transmit communication; no men-
> tion is therefore made of a philosophical friend, or a pleasant
> companion. The seriousness does not arise from any participa-
> tion of calamity, nor the gaiety from the pleasures of the bottle
> ... but [the cheerful man] mingles [as] a mere spectator....
>
> The *pensive* man never loses himself in crowds. . . . /48/
>
> His Cheerfulness is without levity, and his Pensiveness without
> asperity. . . .
>
> No mirth can, indeed, be found in his melancholy; but I am
> afraid that I always meet some melancholy in his mirth. They
> are two noble efforts of imagination.

*Reprinted from *The Well Wrought Urn* (pp. 47-61), copyright, 1947, by Cleanth
Brooks. Reprinted by permission of Harcourt, Brace & World, Inc. and the author.

The passage ends with what is apparently one of the most astonishing *non sequiturs* in criticism. What have the facts given above to do with the fact that the two poems are "noble efforts of imagination"?

Actually they have a great deal to do with it, but Dr. Johnson did not see fit to point out why, and with the critical tools at his disposal, he may very well have had difficulty in doing so. It is characteristic of his honesty and his bluntness that he penetrated so far into the secret, and then rather clumsily appended his concluding judgment.

But Johnson is definitely about the critic's proper job. He inspects the poems—he does not emote over them. And for his failure to connect his observations on the poems with his judgment of their nobility, I hazard the following explanation: Milton is using in these poems something which looks curiously like symbolism, and a symbolism too delicate and indeterminate to be treated in terms of the coarser modes of it such as allegory, for example, with which Dr. Johnson was acquainted.

The typical critic since Johnson has done little more than express his appreciation of the delicious quality of the double poem, feeling perhaps that the beauty of the poem was so obvious as to require no further comment, and the effect given so simple as to render any consideration of architectonics a mere intrusion. This view is based upon a sound consideration of the effectiveness of the poem; but great art is never so simple that it will not repay careful reading, and the result has been that except for communication between admirers of the poem, the "criticism" has been quite useless. Confronted with the skeptic or the honest ignoramus, the admirer has frequently found him- /49/ self embarrassed in attempting to demonstrate that the poem is so fine, or in explaining its difference from the numerous eighteenth-century imitations of it, which, though filled with the same details of landscape, are so wooden and dull.

Professor Tillyard has got much nearer the point in those of his comments which emphasize the element of tone: the poems, he says, are characterized by a "subtle friendliness of tone," and further, Milton displays in them "a perfect social tone." Tillyard has even gone so far as to suggest that the opening passage in "L'Allegro" represents conscious burlesque on Milton's part: "what possessed him," Tillyard asks, "that he should write such bombast? By what strange anticipation did he fall into the manner of the worst kind of eighteenth-century ode? If Milton meant to be noble, he failed dreadfully. If, however, he knew what he was doing, he can only have meant to be funny. And if he meant to be funny, to what end? There is nothing in the rest of the poem that suggests humour — at least of the burlesque sort."

This is all very shrewd. But Professor Tillyard, in his preoccupation with the problem of dating the poems—a matter that has its own importance, certainly—has hardly followed up the implications of his surmise. The alleged burlesque is justified by Tillyard on what are really extrapoetic grounds: the poems were written for an academic audience and the parody on the high-flown style, meant for their amusement, "can perhaps be justified" as the "high spirits of a young man." Tillyard does not relate the justification to the tone of the rest of the double poem, nor to its total effect.

With regard to the symbolism of the poem also, Tillyard has come close to the main matter. In pointing out the close connections between "L'Allegro-Il Penseroso" and Milton's First Prolusion ("Whether Day or Night is the more excellent"), he has indicated how important the day-night contrasts are in determining the general architecture of the poem. But he has not seen that the light-shade imagery amounts to a symbolism and /50/ that this symbolism is related ultimately to the "meaning" of the poem, including its tone.

Precisely how these symbols work — how Milton gives the illusion of full day, dawn, noon, and night, and yet manages to keep both poems bathed in their special quality of coolness, is a matter to be discussed in detail a little later on. For the moment, it is sufficient to prepare for such a discussion by examining a little further Dr. Johnson's observation that the protagonist of both poems is a mere spectator who avoids crowds and who has no companion, and the further observation that mirth and melancholy in this poem "are solitary, silent inhabitants of the breast."

Mirth and melancholy need not be solitary — mirth in particular need not be. Dr. Johnson's reference to the pleasures of the bottle is definitely *not* beside the point; for, if Milton had intended to exploit mere contrast, "L'Allegro" would have been sociable; "Il Penseroso," solitary; "L'Allegro," boisterous; "Il Penseroso," prim and sober. A little consideration, however, will show that Milton could not afford to exploit mere contrast. If he had, the two halves would have been driven poles apart. They would have ceased to be twin halves of *one* poem, for the sense of unity in variety would have been lost. We are almost justified in putting the matter in this way: by choosing the obvious contrast between mirth and melancholy, Milton obligated himself to bring them as close together as possible in their effect on the mind. For the tension between the two choices depends upon their

presentation as choices which can appeal to the same mind; and the
element of choice is worth emphasizing. Such pleasures and such
sorrows as are intruded upon the character — "public," convivial
mirth, or "public" melancholy, a funeral in the family — deprive the
protagonist of conscious choice and render him chosen rather than
choosing. Milton, one feels, is quite as emphatic in his belief that the
aesthetic requires a deliberate act of will as was Immanuel Kant in
insisting that the ethical involves deliberate choice. /51/

It is not for nothing that the "Mountain Nymph, sweet Liberty"
presides over "L'Allegro" and that the "Cherub Contemplation" dom-
inates "Il Penseroso." Yet, as a matter of fact, the "Mountain Nymph"
and the "Cherub," as we shall see, tend to merge into the same figure.

If, under the influence of Milton's later political career, we tend to
give Liberty any political significance, we find her in "L'Allegro" in
very strange company, consorting with

> *Jest and youthful Jollity,*
> *Quips and Cranks, and wanton Wiles,*
> *Nods, and Becks, and Wreathed Smiles ...*
> *Sport that wrinkled Care derides,*
> *And Laughter holding both his sides.*

The petition to Mirth

> *To live with her, and live with thee,*
> *In unreproved pleasures free ...*

indicates, of course, plainly enough why Liberty walks at the right
hand of Mirth: the pleasures are those which are unreproved. They
are, moreover, the pleasures which can be had for the asking — the
pleasure of drifting through the landscape or through the city, and
watching the varying beauties of the landscape or the pageantry of
men. But such pleasures pertain to liberty in another sense also: they
depend upon one's freedom from business appointments and dinner
engagements. One must be able to move along, unhurried and un-
detained, or the spell is broken. The necessity for being at a particular place at a particular time would wreck the cheerful man's day as
described in the poem quite as completely as it would the day of the
pensive man.

Dr. Johnson, always on the alert to ruffle up at the presence of
Milton's somewhat aggressively republican goddess, does not betray
any irritation at the presence of Liberty here. Perhaps he recognized

in her, in spite of the mountain-nymph disguise, the /52/ same deity who presided over some of his own most delightful rambles. And if we find it difficult to associate Dr. Johnson, whose pleasures were uncompromisingly eighteenth-century, with either of Milton's cool and leisurely observers, we might recall such a passage as the following, in which Boswell describes a typical Johnsonian jaunt: "We landed at the Old Swan, and walked to Billingsgate, where we took oars, and moved smoothly along the silver Thames. It was a very fine day. We were entertained with the immense number and variety of ships that were lying at anchor, and with the beautiful country on each side of the river." The parallelism is at once destroyed when talkative Boswell, "the philosophical friends, or . . . pleasant companion," begins again to draw the great man out. But the delight in moving through a busy and fascinating world, leisurely and aimlessly, himself unbusied, was one which Johnson found most attractive. If the indulgence in such pleasures sometimes caused the rigid moralist to reprove himself for idleness, still, idle with such an idleness, he remained to the end. For all their differences over "liberty," the great republican and the great tory find themselves in close agreement here.

I have remarked that the mountain nymph and the cherub tend to merge into the same figure. One can easily see why. The more serious pleasures of Il Penseroso are so obviously "unreproved pleasures free" that the poet does not even need to point out that they are unreproved; yet, on the other hand, they are hardly more "contemplative" than those which delight L'Allegro. The happy man, too, is the detached observer, gliding through his world, a spectator of it, and preserving a certain aesthetic distance between it and himself. It is true that the spectator as the happy man emphasizes the spontaneity, the effortless freedom of his pleasures; and that the more austere observer is more consciously the man dedicated to the contemplative life. But here, as elsewhere in these poems, Milton's oppositions tend to come together.

The cheerful man's day is balanced by the pensive man's day /53/ at every point: a cheery dawn scene played off against a somber evening scene; Elizabethan comedy balanced against Greek tragedy; Lydian airs in antithesis to

> *Such notes as warbled to the string,*
> *Drew Iron tears down Pluto's cheek. . . .*

There is no need to detail them here; they are charming, and everyone knows them. What may be more to the point is to note that the

tendency for these opposites to merge comes out even here. Both
music passages, for example, refer to Orpheus; in "L'Allegro," to an
Orphean strain which might have won Eurydice completely; in "Il
Penseroso," to the Orphean strain played when Orpheus won her only
to lose her. Or, to take another instance, the reference to supernatural
lore in the one case involves *Faery Mab*, the most charming and harm-
less of folklores; in the other, the "unsphering" of

> *The spirit of* Plato *to unfold*
> *What Worlds, or what vast Regions hold*
> *The immortal mind that hath forsook*
> *Her mansion in this fleshly nook:*
> *And of those* Dæmons *that are found*
> *In fire, air, flood or under ground. . . .*

But in neither case are we dealing with vulgar superstition—with the
person in terror of spooks. In "L'Allegro" the superstition is reduced
to a charming and poetic fancy; in "Il Penseroso," it has been ele-
vated to the level of the philosophical imagination.

Even more striking is the tendency for the opposed items to cross
over from their usual antitheses in a fashion which associates the
same object with both mirth and melancholy. Here, the network of
patternings is less obvious, and the instances given here may well be
thought to be merely trivial. Perhaps they are; and yet in poetry so
rich and cunningly contrived as this, we shall probably err less in
putting down apparent rela- /54/ tionships as meant and meaningful
than in assuming that Milton threw materials into the double poem
"every which way," and that the relations among them have no part
in the total effect because we do not consciously associate them with
the effect.

In "Il Penseroso," one of the finest passages is that in which Milton
describes his Platonist toiling on at his studies:

> *Or let my Lamp at midnight hour,*
> *Be seen in some high lonely Towr,*
> *Where I may oft out-watch the* Bear . . .

Yet if "high" and "lonely" seems inevitably associated with the tower,
and the tower itself, the inevitable symbol of the meditative, ascetic
life, one remembers that towers are to be found all through "L'Allegro"
— yet they're associated with anything but lonely solitude. The lark
scares away the dull night by singing "From his watch-towre in the

skies." And again, the next tower that appears is one which is "Boosom'd high in tufted Trees." "Boosom'd" is almost shockingly unascetic. (One is tempted to pursue the parallel with the "Il Penseroso" passage further. There, in the tower he outwatches the stars of the Bear; here the tower contains the "star" which all watch, for "Cynosure" is the constellation of the Lesser Bear.)

Lastly, "Towred" is the adjective which Milton chooses to apply to the cities to which the cheerful man will turn at nightfall after his day in the country—

> *Towred Cities please us then,*
> *And the busie humm of men. . . .*

Or, take another example. The most sociable and crowded scene that occurs in "L'Allegro" is perhaps that in which

> *. . . throngs of Knights and Barons bold,*
> *In weeds of Peace high triumphs hold,*
> *With store of Ladies, whose bright eies*
> *Rain influence, and judge the prise. . . .*

/55/ It is a court scene of some pomp and circumstance. But the only parallel to it in "Il Penseroso" — and Milton has of course provided a parallel — is one of the most poignant of the melancholy delights. The knights have been shifted out of reality into Spenser's Faeryland:

> *And if ought els, great* Bards *beside,*
> *In sage and solemn tunes have sung,*
> *Of Turneys and of Trophies hung;*
> *Of Forests, and inchantments drear,*
> *Where more is meant than meets the ear.*

But the most important device used to bring the patterns of opposites together — to build up an effect of unity in variety — is the use of a basic symbolism involving light. The symbolism never becomes quite explicit, but it is most important, nevertheless, and in the use of it Milton brings all the oppositions of the poem together, and orders and unifies them. I have said that Milton never declares his symbolism explicitly, but he comes very close to it in the preamble of each poem: Melancholy is born "of . . . blackest midnight"; the fancies of Mirth are like the "gay motes that people the Sun Beams." This is more than a broad hint; and to have "L'Allegro" begin with a dawn scene and "Il Penseroso," with an evening scene, emphasizes it.

But "L'Allegro," as we know, is not consistently a daylight poem, just as "Il Penseroso" is not consistently a night poem. The day, for both the cheerful man and the pensive man, embraces the whole round of the twenty-four hours. If both poems are characterized by a leisurely flowing movement as the spectator in each case drifts from pleasure to pleasure, and if in both poems he *is* the detached spectator — not the participant in the world he wanders through — in neither of the poems do we get the flaring sunbeam in which the dust motes swim or the unrelieved blackness of midnight. In both poems the spectator moves through what are predominantly cool half-lights. It is as if the half-light were being used in both poems as a /56/ sort of symbol of the aesthetic distance which the cheerful man, no less than the pensive man, consistently maintains. The full glare of the sun would then symbolize the actual workaday world over which neither the "Mountain Nymph, sweet Liberty" nor the "Cherub Contemplation" presides.

I have said that in this symbolism all the problems of the double poem head up. Let me mention a specific one: the landscape through which the spectator (as cheerful or pensive) moves must seem — even in its variety — cool, inviting, delightful. It must seem subdued to a mood; but more than that, it must present, when seen from every varying vantage-point, an aesthetic object. Yet even in a poem which skirts the *tour de force* as narrowly as this one does, it must seem *real*. It must be a world in which a real sun glares and real people sweat at their work; otherwise, it will seem a reduced world, or even an unreal, paper-thin world. The point is highly important. Milton must not merely, through his selection of materials, rule out the unpleasant or ugly. That is easy enough to do on the mechanical level. His selectivity must operate on a much higher plane: Milton must give the illusion of a real world, and of a full life — the whole round of the day — while at the same time presenting a world which meets at every point L'Allegro's cheer or Il Penseroso's melancholy.

To see how important this is, it is only necessary to recall the "Miltonic" landscapes of Akenside or the Wartons, poets who tend to heap up mechanically the characteristic details of Milton's poem, and yet fail of the characteristic atmosphere.

Since the progression of both "L'Allegro" and "Il Penseroso" is based upon the chronology of the day, Milton's light symbolism comes in naturally (and apparently inevitably), for the clock of the day is the sun; and the allusions to morning, noon, twilight, and moonlight provide Milton all the opportunities which he could wish to develop his symbolism of light and shade.

After the somewhat rhetorical exorcism of Melancholy, "Of /57/ *Cerberus,* and blackest midnight born," Mirth comes in with the morning. The first scene is a dawn scene — sunrise and people going to work: the plowman, the milkmaid, the mower, and the shepherd. But though we see people going to work, we never see them *at* their work, just as we do not ever feel the full glare of the sun. Even after the cottage dinner, when we are told of Phillis that

> *... then in haste her Bowre she leaves,*
> *With* Thestylis *to bind the Sheaves;*
> *Or if the earlier season lead*
> *To the tann'd Haycock in the Mead....*

we do not accompany them to the haycock, nor do we feel the sun which "tans" it. Instead, with "secure delight" we slip with the observer over to one of the "up-land Hamlets" where we watch

> *... many a youth, and many a maid,*
> *Dancing in the Chequer'd shade;*
> *And young and old com forth to play*
> *On a Sunshine Holyday,*
> *Till the live-long day-light fail....*

There is the illusion of a real world and of a daylight world; but the basic scenes of the daylight sequence in "L'Allegro" are dominated by the whistling plowman, the rustics at their noon meal, and the dancing in the "Chequer'd shade." The sunshine is that of a "Sunshine Holyday." Nobody sweats in the world of "L'Allegro" — except the goblin:

> *Tells how the drudging* Goblin *swet,*
> *To ern his Cream-bowle duly set,*
> *When in one night, ere glimps of morn,*
> *His shadowy Flale hath thresh'd the Corn....*

(Perhaps it is overingenious to suggest that in this scene — the only depiction of strenuous activity in the poem — Milton has /58/ "cooled" it off by making the flail "shadowy," by presenting it as part of a night scene, and by making the laborer, not a flesh-and-

blood man, but a goblin. And yet the scene has been carefully patterned: it is balanced by the passage in "Il Penseroso," where the
spectator having taken refuge from the sun, listens

> *While the Bee with Honied thie,*
> *. . . at her flowry work doth sing. . . .*

Goblins and bees are the only creatures presented "at work" in the
two poems.)

If we get merely holiday sunshine in the country-scene sequence of
"L'Allegro," we get, of course, no sunshine at all in the city sequence.
But Milton has attended very carefully to the lighting of the scene
displayed. The "high triumphs" of the knights and barons are presided over by the "bright eies" of the ladies, eyes which "Rain influence." "Rain influence" suggests a star metaphor: the stars were
supposed to rain influence and determine events. The court ceremonial
is succeeded by a wedding ceremony presided over by Hymen with
his "Taper clear." The light in these scenes, then, is starlight or
candlelight, not, to be sure, presented as the actual physical lighting
of the scenes, but certainly insinuated into the mood of the scenes.
The "thronged" scenes of "L'Allegro" are thus softened — the aesthetic distance from which they are viewed is thus indicated — just
as the scenes of physical work have been softened and pushed back
from the immediate presence of the observer.

The common-sense reader who distrusts the ingenious and wants
his poetry to be explicit, declared, and forthright, may well ask why,
if all this elaborate handling of the lighting is going on, Milton has to
handle it so indirectly. Why doesn't Milton declare himself? But
Milton does — at least with regard to the central element of the
symbol, the association of the raw glare of the sun with the workaday world. In "Il Penseroso," when the showery morning has passed
and the sun has broken forth, the speaker says: /59/

> *And when the Sun begins to fling*
> *His flaring beams, me Goddes bring*
> *To arched walks of twilight groves,*
> *And shadows brown that* Sylvan *loves*
> *Of Pine, or monumental Oake,*
> *Where the rude Ax with heaved stroke,*
> *Was never heard the Nymphs to daunt,*
> *Or fright them from their hallow'd haunt.*
> *There in close covert by som Brook,*

> *Where no profaner eye may look,*
> *Hide me from Day's garish eie....*

We are not told in so many words that the sun ("Day's . . . eie")
is one of the "profaner" eyes; but it is "garish"; and it is associated
definitely with the "heaved stroke." The pensive man withdraws
from both—to the "twilight groves" where he may hear only the
"work" of the bee—"flowry work," at which the bee sings—labor
which is a part of nature itself. But the cheerful man too, as we have
seen, has been kept out of "Day's garish eie" almost as completely
as has Il Penseroso himself.

On the other hand, "Il Penseroso" avoids "blackest midnight" too.
And at this point we are prepared to take up Tillyard's point about
the burlesque style of the passage in which Melancholy is dismissed.
The reprehension of Melancholy as loathsome, and the identification
of her with the blackness of midnight are associated with a consciously
stilted rhetoric which forms an ironical contrast with the freer and
more casual rhythms in which the pensive man's actual experience of
melancholy is expressed. It is the most delicate kind of qualification
that a poet can give. For those who feel with Tillyard that the
opening *is* bombastic, the presence of the bombast thus becomes
meaningful. Melancholy as actually experienced by the pensive man
is not a monstrosity at all. In contrast to her "literary" and abstract
caricature, the actual goddess moves in /60/ a solid and "real" world,
a beautiful world, and not a world of midnight black.

The poem has her come in with evening into a scene dominated by
the moon. But even when the pensive man goes within doors and
the moonlight is shut out, there are the "glowing Embers" which
"Teach light to counterfeit a gloom." Midnight itself, when it is
mentioned, is relieved by the speaker's studious lamp, and above the
tower the stars are shining:

> *Or let my Lamp at midnight hour,*
> *Be seen in som high lonely Towr,*
> *Where I may oft out-watch the* Bear....

The night scene here balances the starlight and candlelight of its companion scene in "L'Allegro," with starlight and lamplight—though
the stars here are not the eyes of brilliant women which "Rain
influence, and judge the prise" but the cold, watchful stars of Ursa
Major.

More important still, the sequence which follows, with its references to Plato, "Gorgeous Tragedy," Chaucer, and the other "great *Bards*," emphasizes the light accorded to the "inward eye," and thus provides a concrete realization of the paradox hinted at earlier in the poem: that the black of night, "staid Wisdoms hue," is merely a necessary veil to conceal a brightness which is in reality too intense for human sight.

This, of course, is the point which Milton was to make years later when he wrote his *Paradise Lost*, where, addressing the celestial light, he says:

> *Shrine inward, and the mind through all her powers*
> *Irradiate, there plant eyes, all mist from thence*
> *Purge and disperse, that I may see and tell*
> *Of things invisible to mortal sight.*

When "Il Penseroso" was being written, that day was far in the future, and it is not my purpose to suggest that the poem gives a calculated foresight of that sterner time to come. What one /61/ may fairly say, however, is that the light symbolism, used so powerfully, though unobstrusively, in these earlier poems, was perfectly consonant with Milton's thinking, and was to emerge later in the great poem quite explicitly.

Actually, the connection of the life of contemplation with the higher life, and of the shades associated with melancholy with the brightest visions (though unearthly visions) is made quite explicitly at the end of "Il Penseroso." This concluding passage, by the way, has no parallel in the twin poem: "Il Penseroso" is twenty-four lines longer than its companion piece.

Here the secular life is made to pass over into the religious—the semipaganism of the "Genius of the Wood" frankly gives way to Christianity, and the measure of aesthetic distance with which the world has been consistently viewed is extended into the hermit's avowed withdrawal from the secular world altogether. The light symbolism accommodates itself to the change:

> *... storied Windows richly dight,*
> *Casting a dimm religious light.*

The pensive man is now bathed neither in midnight nor in the moted sunbeam. The daylight of the senses, dimmed and enriched by the

storied windows, has been brought nearer to darkness, and yet at
the same time prepared for the vision of the inward eye:

> *Dissolve me into extasies,*
> *And bring all Heav'n before mine eyes.*

Is the light "dimm" because religious, or religious because "dimm"?
Or is it paradoxically dim, though religious—dim to the physical eye,
though actually the proper light for one who would have the vision
too insupportably bright for human sight to receive? To unravel
these questions is to recapitulate the entire symbolism of the two
poems. Suffice it to say that the collocation, if it seems inevitable,
seems so because of Milton's cunning development of the light passages
throughout the poems.

Kester Svendsen

Milton's "L'Allegro" and "Il Penseroso"*

Empson's dismissal of "L'Allegro" and "Il Penseroso" as "ponderous trifles" in his review of Brooks' *The Well Wrought Urn* (*Sewanee Review*, 1947, LV, 691) and Brooks' acceptance of the disparagement of his Milton chapter if not of the poems possibly arose from the fact that the light and shade symbolism stressed by Brooks is static. It can be shown, however, that the dynamics of the twin poem, and hence the structural unity, derive not so much from this symbolism exploited by Brooks as from the progressive emphasis in both parts on images of sound and music. These culminate in the very passage of "inward seeing" upon which Brooks concludes his analysis:

> There let the pealing Organ blow,
> To the full voic'd Quire below,
> In Service high, and Anthems clear,
> As may with sweetness, through mine ear,
> Dissolve me into extasies,
> And bring all Heav'n before mine eyes.

Brooks refers to the Orpheus parallels and one or two related matters, but without capitalizing upon their significance. A review of the sound images will emphasize the real meaning of the Anglican ritual near the end of "Il Penseroso."

In contrast to the shrieks of the raven in the prologue to "L'Allegro," the cheerful man begins his day to the lark's singing and the cock's

---

*Reprinted from *Explicator*, VIII (May, 1950), item 49, by permission of *The Explicator*, copyright Virginia Commonwealth University, and the executrix of the author's estate. [Note to student: Since the *Explicator* does not use page numbers, refer to item 49.]

lively din. He listens to the hounds and the horn echoing through the wood. The workers are similarly characterized: the plowman whistles, the milkmaid sings, the mower scrapes his whetsone across the scythe, and even the shepherd is shown telling his story (or counting his sheep!). The dancers in the "Chequer'd shade" are invited there by bells and rebecks. They then tell stories, ending with the goblin who flings out of doors before "the first Cock his Mattin rings." The daylight part of the poem is framed by this and the earlier mention of the cock's lively din. Then "to bed they creep By whispering Windes soon lull'd asleep." Next is the picture of knights and ladies so acutely explicated by Brooks; but it is introduced by two lines in which the contrasting towered cities are described only by mention of "the busy Humm of men." Shakespeare is presented as a superior sort of lark, warbling his native woodnotes; and the poem concludes with a eulogy to music married to verse in which sound untwists "all the chains that ty The hidden soul of harmony." The cheerful man is never dramatized as singing or talking, but always as listening to or being affected by the talk, the noise, the music. The secret of the harmony in the aesthetic surfaces upon which he touches is here hinted at but not developed.

In "Il Penseroso" Melancholy is invited to bring along the Cherub Contemplation and "mute Silence," unless (and the condition continues the emphasis on music in "L'Allegro") the nightingale will sing. She is described as if the terms were appositives: "Most musicall, most melancholy"; and the pensive man woos to "hear her even-Song." If he misses her, then he walks in the cool half-lights, looks at the moon, and listens to the far-off curfew sound (which pairs with the distant echoing of hounds and horn at the beginning of the cheerful man's day). In the passage where Brooks' half-lights are most explicit (the glowing embers teaching "light to counterfeit a gloom"), the pensive man hears the cricket on the hearth or "the Belmans drousie charm." The line itself illustrates the power of music. "Charm" means both song, as the editors have remarked, and incantation, as the line following it indicates. The effect of the sound and sense here is less obvious but structurally more functional than that in the familiar sound-image "Over some wide-water'd shoar. Swinging slow with sullen roar," because it looks back to the power of music in the conclusion of "L'Allegro" and forward to the conclusion of "Il Penseroso." The pensive man is made drowsy, but he outwatches the Bear in contemplation. As he does he wishes that the "sad Virgin" might invoke Orpheus, whose notes, "warbled to the string," suggest an identification with the nightingale, for they are

most musical (i.e., most powerful, in making Hell grant love's request)
and most melancholy (in drawing tears down Pluto's cheek). The
knights and tourneys of Brooks' world of unreality are then introduced, like those of the world of reality, by a reference to sound,
here the "sage and solemn tunes" where "more is meant than meets
the ear."

Further along, the piping of winds and the rustling of leaves are
contrasted; and when the pensive man seeks refuge from the flaring
sun, he does so in a grove where the nymphs have not been frightened
away by the sound of the rude ax. The bee, which parallels the goblin
in "L'Allegro" as the only worker, is like the goblin associated with
sound. The bee sings, and the consort between her singing and the
murmuring of the waters is, like the bellman's charm, an inducement
to sleep. This time the pensive man sleeps, but wishes to wake to
music sent by some spirit or genius of the wood. He concludes with a
plea in which religious music becomes the agency of his identification
of himself with the unknowable—the goal of the mystic. In the lines
"But let my due feet never fail, To walk the studious Cloysters pale,"
the word "but" has the force of "in any event," so that the whole
passage which follows becomes a climax to the general experience
of the two poems and a contradiction of the special request for music
from the pagan genius of the wood. It is as if the pensive man were
recalling himself from what is after all only a myth and a foreshadow-
ing. He wishes to hear the organ and the choir in such harmony as
may with sweetness put him into the mystic's ecstasy and bring all
Heaven before his eyes. The organ music is not distant, like the hound
and horn and the curfew sound, but close. It is not from the world
of unreality or make-believe, like the Orpheus music, but real, like
the bellman's charm, and more significant. The mystic vision is
achieved not merely by contemplation but specifically through the
power of music. The two motifs of light and sound have been played
off against each other throughout the poems. That tension is now
resolved in their parallel expression here, with sound the effective
force: the pensive man will see all Heaven before his eyes because of
the music taken in through his ear. This religious experience contrasts
with the pagan myth at the conclusion of "L'Allegro," but is in the
same continuum, as it were.

With the possible exception of the reference to the goddess Melancholy as a nun (which is ambiguous; Marlowe called Hero a nun),
there is no allusion to Christianity in either poem until this passage.
Here the contrast is unmistakable but not irreconcilable; the many

references to sound and in particular to music build toward this conclusion, so that structurally it is the end of a progressive development
within both poems. The poet moves from communication through
pagan mythology to the experience of Christian mysticism induced by
Christian religious music. The merging of the two poems, so clearly
demonstrated by Brooks from the light symbolism, is rendered more
significant by this inner movement based on sound and harmony. For
the pensive man in his ecstasy experiences what Milton said in the
nativity hymn could happen through the "holy Song" of the spheres
and the angels. This force of musical harmony suggests further that
feature of the Renaissance world-view in which man's perfect inner
harmony would be correspondent to the harmony of nature and
especially to that of the spheres. The two streams of imagery, light
and sound, touch continually and reinforce each other. An awareness
of their parallel function, the one static, the other dynamic, might
have bolstered Brooks' conviction that the poems are not ponderous
trifles, as Empson called them, but works of art well worth critical
examination.

J. Milton French

Light and Work in "L'Allegro" and "Il Penseroso"*

Professor Cleanth Brooks's essay on Milton's "L'Allegro" and "Il Penseroso" in *The Well Wrought Urn* (1947), reprinted with a few minor alterations in his edition of *Poems of Mr. John Milton* (1951), is a fresh and interesting approach about which it may seem ungrateful to raise questions. But in view of its wide dissemination it is perhaps equally wrong not to question a few interpretations of facts.

I shall not discuss differences of opinion. These are inevitable in our judgments of the arts, and healthy. For example, I doubt whether many students of Milton would agree that "except for communication between admirers of the poem, the 'criticism' has been quite useless." So sweeping an annihilation of all previous criticism seems both unreasonable and self-defeating, since, if it is true, the chances are about 1,000 to 1 that Mr. Brooks's own criticism will soon fall into the same discard. Again, Mr. Brooks's perplexity over the fact that a tower is the symbol of asceticism in one poem but not in the other, and his pretended shock at Milton's naughty use of the word "Boosom'd" to describe towers and battlements in "L'Allegro" (line 78) may seem to be difficult reactions to have worked up. But these are matters of opinion, in which everyone has a right to his choice.

Some of Mr. Brooks's criticisms, however, rest on misinterpretations of the facts of the poems. Though we can agree to disagree as to the propriety of "Boosom'd," there is only one right answer to the question whether or not the word occurs in the poem. One is /124/ a question of judgment, the other of fact. I should like in this paper to confine myself to a few questions about the facts of the poems.

*Reprinted from *South Atlantic Quarterly*, LVIII (Winter, 1959), 123-27, by permission of Duke University Press.

We may consider first Mr. Brooks's comment that Milton "manages to keep both poems bathed in their special quality of coolness." As he puts it later, "In both poems the spectator moves through what are predominantly cool half-lights," which are a "symbol of the aesthetic distance which the cheerful man, no less than the pensive man, consistently maintains."

Presumably this statement means that the poet, in both poems, avoided either bright light or complete blackness, using always shades between these extremes. We may test the accuracy of this interpretation in two ways: by studying the words and phrases to see whether they are all actually limited to half-lights, and by analyzing general impressions. The second method is more difficult but necessary. As for the words themselves, some certainly fulfil Mr. Brooks's requirements: "dull night" ("L'Allegro," line 42 in Milton's *Poems,* 1645), "dappled dawn" (44), "labouring clouds" (74), "Chequer'd shade" (96), "glimmering Bowres" ("Il Penseroso," 27), "secret shades" (28), "wandring Moon" (67), "fleecy cloud" (72), "glowing Embers through the room/Teach light to counterfeit a gloom" (79-80), "civil-suited Morn . . . Cherchef't in a comly Cloud" (122-125), "twilight groves,/And shadows brown" (133-134), and of course especially our old friend, "dimm religious light" (160), a phrase so familiar that it may have given rise to the whole idea. On the other hand, there are a number of examples of extreme light or darkness: "blackest midnight" ("L'Allegro," 2), "brooding darkness" (6), "dark *Cimmerian* desert" (10), "the great Sun begins his state/Rob'd in flames and Amber light" (60-61), "Sunshine Holyday" (98), "live-long day-light" (99), "Sun Beams" ("Il Penseroso," 8), "rugged brow of night" (58), "the Sun begins to fling/His flaring beams" (131-132), and the "Day's garish eie" (141). Quantitatively, the second group is not much short of the first. Qualitatively, if the original criticism has any force whatever, it must rest on consistency throughout the poems, and the existence of these terms imperils its force.

These are statistical factors. What is our general impression of the two poems? To some extent this too is a matter of personal /125/ judgment, where any man is entitled to give his opinion. Mr. Brooks thinks the general effect is of half-light. I would agree as to "Il Penseroso," but not as to "L'Allegro," which seems to me to present a bright, sunny, daytime canvas in the daytime section of the poem. Some of the time, of course, the speaker of the poem, like any normal man, seeks the shade to escape the heat of the sun. But this fact seems a testimony to the brightness of the scene. I can find no distant, aesthetic, aloof coolness.

Theoretically, this matter of light is the central point of the whole essay, since the title is "The Light Symbolism" in the poems. Actually, other matters occupy nearly half the essay. But Mr. Brooks has more to say of the light than I have indicated. "If we get merely holiday sunshine in the country-scene sequence of 'L'Allegro,' we get, of course, no sunshine at all in the city sequence," meaning "Il Penseroso." The "merely holiday" modification refers to the supposed "cooling" effect of the goblin's "shadowy" flail, so described because it is used at night. Probably this is the reason why we read that "the cheerful man too, as we have seen, has been kept out of 'Day's garish eie' almost as completely as has Il Penseroso himself." But except for the occasional "Chequer'd shade" which any sensible person would look for after being out in the hot sun during the morning, it is hard to see any justification in "L'Allegro" for this allegation. The cheerful man moves from his sunny window through the fields, watching the plowman, the milkmaid, the mower, and the shepherd, through pastures and past mountains and towers and cottages, through the hayfield, to the upland hamlets where there is dancing in the shade and play in the sun, and finally to evening and night activities. How any watcher could observe all these sights (except by some trickery, which certainly would be beneath Milton's code of honor) without spending a good deal of time in full sunshine ("Day's garish eie") I cannot understand. Any such interpretation seems forced.

Second, Mr. Brooks states that the pleasures brought by the Mountain Nymph, sweet Liberty, "depend upon one's freedom from business appointments and dinner engagements." Surely he is pulling our leg in this section, warning us not to take our criticism—or ourselves —too seriously. Of course he is right. The speakers in both poems, like the author, did not have to spend eight hours a day /126/ at the desk. But did Mr. Brooks mean to distinguish Milton's poems in this respect from others of his day? Are the pictures of England in the poems of Jonson, Shakespeare, Donne, Marvell, Herbert, Vaughan, and other poets of the age seen through the eyes of drudges who punch a time-clock? If they are, most of us will have to learn to read them anew. If they are not, there seems to be no particular point in this criticism, since Milton merely follows the custom of his time.

Third (and closely related to the preceding), Mr. Brooks tells us that "though we see people going to work, we never see them *at* their work, just as we do not ever feel the full glare of the sun." Again, "Nobody sweats in the world of 'L'Allegro'—except the goblin," and, as he adds later, the bees. Now even though we may grant that these two poems are not primarily descriptions of sweatshops, how much

poetry is? One could perhaps collect an anthology of verse describing
heavy labor, but one would have to sweat himself a bit in the process.
Poetry, at least before our day, has usually not been concerned chiefly
with manual labor but rather with either thought or emotion or both.
Chaucer, Shakespeare, Donne, Dryden, Pope, Wordsworth, Keats,
Tennyson—passages of sweat and grime in their works are the exception. Milton follows the same pattern. These two poems of his, like
most of the writings of Jonson, Herbert, and Crashaw, to take three
of the first contemporary names which come to mind, have little
connection with hard physical labor. The criticism is therefore almost
meaningless.

At the same time, there is more work in the poems than Mr. Brooks
implies. Though not underlined, it pervades both poems. The plowman, the milkmaid, the mower, the shepherd, the huntsmen, the
"busie humm of men," the minister at the wedding, Phillis and
Thestylis, the wielder of the rude ax, and the bellman are all active
workers as certainly as are the goblin and the bee. They may enjoy
their work, some of them, but presumably that fact should not
disqualify them. But these are only a few of the workers. Numerous
others have perhaps escaped notice because we enjoy their work so
much that we forget the labor involved. The actors in the plays, for
example, are really working, as any member of the theatrical pro-
fession will testify. Musicians, again, at least in the opinion of their
union officials, are working when they play. If it is stretching /127/ a
point to include Orpheus and Cynthia and Philomel, the lark, the
cock, the hounds, the pensive nun, and Philomel in this group, they
are at least doing their proper, regular tasks. In short, the statement
that "Goblins and bees are the only creatures presented 'at work' in
the two poems" is about as wide of the mark as it could be.

Finally, Mr. Brooks raises the question whether the light of the
church windows in "Il Penseroso" is dim because it is religious (line
160), religious because it it dim, or physically dim to allow spiritual
vision. His answer is that "To unravel these questions is to recapitulate
the entire symbolism of the two poems." But the answer is actually
quite simple. We may perhaps discard the first two alternatives as
merely playful, since obviously neither condition, dim or religious,
is a *cause* of the other. The third alternative is based on a wrong
assumption: that Milton had a choice of all grades of light in his
church and selected dim light for some abstruse reason of his own.
But of course all that he did was to reproduce what he found in any
normal church of his day. The heavily colored, narrow, high windows
naturally excluded most of the outdoor light, and were intended by

the designers of the churches to do so for several reasons, one being
that named. They usually do the same today. But to ask the question
at all as if it implied an intentional manipulation by Milton is like
asking whether he has stopped beating his wife. Once we grant that
the pensive man should go into the church at all, then we should
naturally expect him to find a dim religious light inside. If he should
find blazing sunshine instead, then Milton would really have been
pulling the strings.

   To summarize, (1) the light is not uniformly shaded but ranges
from blazing sunshine to blackest midnight; (2) freedom from business appointments and dinner engagements is natural but irrelevant;
(3) the poems are full of workers; and (4) the dim religious light
is natural, not manipulated. The magic of Milton's poems is both
too powerful and too subtle to be explained by any such frail devices
as these. It is to be hoped that Mr. Brooks may some day offer us a
more satisfying analysis.

Eleanor Tate

From Milton's "L'Allegro" and "Il Penseroso"-Balance, Progression, or Dichotomy?*

In "L'Allegro" Milton's world seems close to a small-scale vision of the ideal, green comic world, the world of *As You Like It,* for example. This he sets against other unreal dream worlds: the chivalric past, the classical world of myth, the fairy tale world of Queen Mab and the goblins, and finally Shakespeare's world of romantic comedy. The chivalric world is introduced in ll. 59-62, where the poet describes the sun at the great eastern gate, attended by "The clouds in thousand Liveries dight." It enters again in ll. 77-80 in the "Towers and Battlements" passage, and in the description of the cities, ll. 117-130. The rustics—Corydon, Thyrsis, Phyllis, and Thestylis—represent the classical pastoral world. The Queen Mab allusion takes on some complexity, for this fairy world is an escape world even within the idealized green world—it is the story world of the country folk, in which goblins do their work at night. Milton's idealized world is a surface world, even as that of Shakespeare's romantic comedies. Yet, as in Shakespeare, things are going on beneath the surface, and we are not allowed to forget reality completely—it nudges us periodically, reminding that this is only a dream. Although "loathed Melancholy" is dismissed in the introduction, "wrincled Care" is present deriding Sport. The poet desires to live with Mirth in "unreproved pleasures free," the very word *unreproved* suggesting an awareness of censure. The Lark awakens in "in spight [despite] of sorrow." The liveried mountains labor and need rest. And the reference to Jonson undercuts slightly the more enlarged reference to Shakespeare's pastoral world. The "Sweet Liberty" has become wantonness in the sexual imagery

---

*Reprinted from *Modern Language Notes*, LXXVI (November, 1961), 585-90, copyright © The Johns Hopkins Press. Only pp. 588-590 are reprinted here.

of ll. 137-40. And even though he wants to believe otherwise, there is the suggestion in this same passage that to give oneself to the illusion, however appealing, is to become lost in a maze. He acknowledges with regret that he has been describing "such sights as youthful Poets dream /On Summer eeves by haunted stream" (ll. 129-30). They are illusory. Like Keats after him, who longed to "die a death / Of luxury," Milton desired to escape from the "eating Cares" of the world (still present at the end of the poem—l. 135) and be immersed "in soft *Lydian* Aires, / Married to immortal verse." I would ques-
/589/ tion the footnote on these lines in the Merritt Hughes edition of Milton, stating that Milton ignored "the traditional prejudice against Lydian music as morally enervating."[1] Rather, the speaker of the poem is really deceiving himself concerning this music. Like Keats again, he has to discover that this is not the way to untwist "all the chains that ty / The hidden soul of harmony" (ll. 143-4). Incidentally, I feel that this whole passage expresses quite an intense personal desire on Milton's part. In l. 129 (quoted above), part of this same passage, he has made his first reference to the poet. The line forms an unobtrusive transition to a central theme of the poems, the role of the poet. He soon becomes more personal and direct. His union with Mirth is, he trusts, a marriage to "immortal verse." Milton has dedicated himself to poetry, desiring to awaken the great poet Orpheus, even. And it is rather interesting in this first reference to this myth that it is Orpheus rather than Pluto that the poet wishes to impress. He aspires to a place in the ranks of the greatest poets. The doubt of the way he has chosen, however, ironically persists in the *if* of the last two lines:

> These delights, if thou canst give,
> Mirth with thee, I mean to live.

In "Il Penseroso" the poet rejects the "fancies" and "hovering dreams" for reality, the world of pain and tragedy (1.97). The poet's function takes on divine and prophetic connotations. In contrast to "L'Allegro," this second poem is full of religious images: Melancholy treated as a Nun, her "rapt soul," the "Spare Fast" of the gods, "*Joves* Altar," the contemplative life, the poet's tower or hermit's retreat in which he becomes a watchman. Seemingly the "immortal mind" of the universe has forsaken the world of mankind and Daemon powers have taken control (ll. 90-6). The divine spirit of poetry seems

---

[1]*Complete Poems and Major Prose* (New York, 1957), p. 71.

asleep in the world. This poem, too, contains an Orpheus reference, but here, in contrast to "L'Allegro," the poet is concerned with the influence of his poetry on Hell itself. The emphasis has shifted from desire for personal fame and recognition to his influence as an inspired poet-prophet. The dream of this poem becomes the "mysterious dream" of prophetic vision. *Mysterious* no doubt is used in a Scriptural sense, referring to the hidden truths of divine revelation. "Il Penseroso" concludes with the poet seeking the mystical experience /590/ of union with God. He rejects illusion; by an act of will he submits to the pain of life and gives himself to thought and religious contemplation

> Till old experience do attain
> To something like Prophetic strain.
> (ll. 173-4)

Don Cameron Allen

The Search for the Prophetic Strain: "L'Allegro" and "Il Penseroso"*

It should not pass unnoticed that there is a concealed unity in *The Shepheardes Calender* established by the confused meditations of the new poet who is attempting to plot the maze of life before he treads it. Snared by the tradition and by a sensibility of purpose, he inquires of himself the way. Is it love, or art, or religion? This is no easy question for him to answer because the intricacy of paths cross and recross, hindering immensely the prospect of direction. The troubadours, whose descendant Spenser was, had found the road through the grace of sophistry and the merit of compromise; but in 1580, the troubadour was only a chivalric memory, and the question, answered finally in the *Hymnes* and the *Amoretti,* was again an open one.

A half century later, Milton had a far easier choice. He had tuned his harp in Sion and not in Toulouse; hence one of the ways, the sweet and gallant course of love, was not for his walking. He had his Dantesque hour on that spring day, memorialized in the seventh elegy, when he saw the girl who surpassed in loveliness all her companions. She vanished and was never seen again. "Interea misero quae iam mihi sola placebat / Ablata est, oculis non reditura meis." The incident is familiar, but the eventuation is not. She becomes no vaporous embodiment of an ideal, a Beatrice, a Rosalind. She is not only erased from the book of memory, but she and her kind will shortly become like Amaryllis with whom one *sports* or like Neaera who traps her lovers in the uncouth *tangles* of her hair. /4/ For

---

*Reprinted from *The Harmonious Vision: Studies in Milton's Poetry*. Baltimore: The Johns Hopkins Press, 1954, pp. 3-23 by permission.

Milton, dedicated to other services, romantic love cannot be even the literary artifice that it was for some of his loveless contemporaries.

The choice of ways was made still simpler for Milton because he early decided to combine the other two courses; so the paths of dissent became for him a kingsway of agreement. When I write this I know that I am begging for disapproval, since it has become customary to observe that Milton, though theologically learned, was deficient in religious feeling. Southwell, Herbert, Crashaw, I am told, knew God, whereas Milton attempted only to explain him. A series of critics have informed me that he was majorly a theological poet who festooned the abstract concepts of divinity with the metallic metaphors of a Latinized style. Of the inward fierceness that is generated by overwhelming religious experience he had nothing. Such is the conclusion of those who think of religion as a kind of emotional experience similar in its appetite to swooning at a melodrama or drooling over an inhaler of Napoleon brandy. Milton, even as a young man, knew better than this; he knew that God thought eternally without the obstruction of emotional shivers. This was his image of the deity and in this image he chose to dwell, to shape thereby the route that would best lead him to this end. The nature of this route is partly revealed in "L'Allegro" and "Il Penseroso," and they must be read, not as two poems, but rather as a single utterance on an exalted proposal.

Johnson unbent enough to describe these poems as "noble efforts of the imagination"; and though he thought of them as representing the character and activities of the "chearful" and the pensive man, he noticed that both men were lonely. "Both Mirth and Melancholy are solitary, silent inhabitants of the breast that neither receive nor transmit communications; no mention is therefore made of a philosophical friend or a pleasant companion." Johnson is right; the poet is as lonely as God and to some extent he shares in God's stasis. He may walk "not unseen" in "L'Allegro" and "unseen" in "Il Penseroso" but there is practically no other motion in him. The poems /5/ were written in a room and to a large degree they remain in a room, although imaginatively they seem to be out-of-doors. They are permeated by a sense of wall; they have an aloofness and a detachment from the wider dimensions of the world that is symbolically described in them and from the vigorous activities of the men who people this world. There is tribulation enough in the web of the verse, but it is of an intellectual sort and it is characterized by the occasional syntactical confusions that trouble the reader as the poet himself was troubled. In spite of this, there broods over the poems a dominating stillness as if the poet were already at the state of satisfaction that the concluding lines of the second poem predict.

Although these are the poems of a solitary man, they anticipate an even greater quest for creative solitude. "L'Allegro" begins in a morning room where the windows are blinded by vines; "Il Penseroso" ends in a church as the light of the rising sun is muted by painted glass, "casting a dim religious light." The final expectation of the meditating poet is the supreme privacy of the hermit's "mossy cell." We pass from room to room through the twilight of the human imagination. "As when the Sun new ris'n / Looks through the Horizontal misty Air / Shorn of his Beams." Broad day pours its light through only the first forty lines of "L'Allegro," but even here it is obscured by clouds, by smoke, and by "the Chequer'd shade." "Hide me from Day's garish eye," cries the poet as dawn begins to sift through the leaves in "Il Penseroso," where the moon at her zenith measures out her light "through a fleecy cloud." The colors of both poems are grays, browns, subdued blues, lighted blacks, and, almost as we watch, we see them veil the ephemeral numerals of the finite world clock. From lark to nightingale, from dawn to nightset, the shadow moves circularly on the dial, tracing the procession of common experience. These temporal episodes have been variously admired as constituting the essence of the poem; yet they are mainly clichés of only ancillary importance. They have a total symbolic value, but in their separateness they are simply an alphabet of common experience easily recited by anyone. /6/

Milton certainly knew that he was not the first poet to select affective episodes to expound the turning of the earth. Many of his poetic counters, as the annotators have found, had been used before. The lark, the cock, the nightingale, the bee, the cricket had long been loud as sentinels of the day or as nocturnal musicians. The monody of living waters is a traditional accomplice of Sleep and Dreams. The plowman, the mower, the milkmaid, the shepherd had formerly followed their trades not only in literary but in artistic accounts of the hours, the months, the year. These *impresas* are so constantly representative of the imagery of day and night that a contemporary of Milton's would have acknowledged them at once and added many others.

Milton himself used some of them in the first prolusion and he knew of others: the capering she-goat, the marigold, the rose—creatures of day; then those pejorative symbols of the evil aspect of night: thieves, murderers, goblins, ghosts, owls, and hags. Interesting as they are, these reiterated devices are not the main source of the poems' virtue.

They are some of the instruments in the orchestra, but in themselves they are not the music which is produced by their ascending confluence. According to the rules of epic variety they will be used later for the descriptions of day and night in the fourth and fifth books of *Paradise Lost*. Then they will be refined and implicative to the degree that they will have a more intimating and a more organic containment. They will in this final appearance not seem so unattached, so capable of desultory rearrangement as they do in this first performance to him who reads them out of the pattern; in fact, they will gain in poetic intensity in the epic because this apparent earlier separateness will seem to be erased. Yet this illusive separateness is produced not so much from lack of literary skill as from the agony of a creative struggle. To say this is to negate all of my previous remarks about the solitary quietness which is the first impression that I abstract from the poems, but the negation is not real because this impression of struggle provides me with a synthetic antithesis that permits me to discern a new basic tone. /7/

The nonhortatory section of "L'Allegro" begins with the song of the lark and the crowing of the cock; that of "Il Penseroso" with a poetic essay on the nightingale. In Milton's age the three birds were symbols of vigilance. The summoner lark was the emblem of the daily resurrection of the world. The cock that brought the sun up and that marked the hours of the night with his crowing was the symbol of watchfulness and for this reason was reproduced in effigy on spires. The nightingale was alleged in the books of the ornithologists to be sleepless. The notion of the alert man seems to me to be stronger in these poems than that of the cheerful or the pensive man; it is the other side of the quiet solitary and it is the necessary component of the subsurface struggle. The vigilance indicated is not one of open activity; it is not a matter of constant gesture or violent flourishes. The poet is always awake, but this awakeness is disguised by the divine stillness of thought. His mind does the body's labor. There is in neither poem a place for sleep. The poet of "Il Penseroso" seeks repose after daybreak, but the poet of "L'Allegro" rises with the sun. The slumber that is sought is not real sleep; it is a poetic sleep filled with "strange mysterious dreams." This is an important point in the total exegesis of the poems and I shall return to it. For the moment it can be observed that as "wanton heed" and "giddy cunning" qualify the musical pleasures of "L'Allegro," so, perhaps, "alert quiet" is a tone that possesses both poems.

With this statement, if it has not been apparent before, I join the party of those who see these poems as deeply serious and take issue with the theses of Tillyard[1] and to some extent with those of Brooks.[2] I am ready to agree that the first prolusion contains the seeds of the poems and I am ready to assume that the poems came to flower in *Paradise Lost,* but I cannot think of the poems as metrical annexes to the prolusion from which they are so different in purpose. The prolusion has the "social tone" that Tillyard and Brooks find in the poems. I look for this tone in vain, and I expect that they have unwit- /8/ tingly transferred it from the prose. In "L'Allegro," which must be the most social poem of the two, there is nothing so familiar as the *"academici,"* or *"pace vestra,"* or *"causam dignemini meam vestris ornare suffragiis,"* or the many other suggestions of the second person plural that we hear in the prolusion. The plowman may be "near at hand," but he is so intent on his plowing and his whistling that he does not salute the poet nor the poet him. We are not sure that the beauty really lives in the castle; certainly, if she does, she is unknown to the stranger poet. The stock Arcadian characters are observed from a safe distance or overheard at their chatter while the poet takes his ease at a rural inn. He does not join in the haying, the dancing, or the tale-telling. In the city he is also a spectator if the things that he witnesses there are real at all; this I can say because Milton tells me that the events described are such "as youthful poets dream." He attends the theater; he listens to concerts. His interest in men and their daily affairs is passive, almost disinterested.

Either I or the poems are devoid of humor, for I cannot read them as *jeux d'esprit* or burlesques. The hortatory beginnings are bombastic, but they are no more bombastic than public prayer. In "L'Allegro," after the worst sort of melancholy is dismissed, Euphrosyne, chief of the graces, is invited to attend the poet because as a mythologist Milton knew that she was the companion of the Horae. He rectifies her ancestry, making her, in the Baconian fashion, a kind of nature myth and as such more readily accessible to men. With her he associates the oread Liberty, the "Mountain Nymph." The qualification suggests political liberty, but I agree with Brooks that Milton intends the sylvan lady to stand for something larger than this though I cannot share Brooks' special materialistic interpretation. To any man of the seventeenth century *liberty* meant what *libertas* meant to an ancient: *manumission.* What has enslaved the poet, we must ask, and from what does he desire to be freed? "Hence loathed Melancholy / Of Cerberus and blackest midnight born." The poems

[1]*The Miltonic Setting* (New York, 1949), 1-28.
[2]*The Well Wrought Urn* (New York, 1947), 47-61.

contain the traces of a struggle, but they also describe a progress
from an enslaving dissatisfaction to an ultimate /9/ gratification. The
original distemper is implied in the lines subsequent to the invocation
of "L'Allegro."

> Then to come *in spite of sorrow*,
> And at my window bid good morrow.

Why is the poet (for it is the poet and certainly not the lark) sad at
the commencement of his progress, at the outset of the struggle?
I cannot pretend to know, but a juxtaposition of images in the center
of the poem may be important.

Having rapidly presented the reader with a stereotyped catalogue
of dawn events, Milton writes,

> Mountains on whose barren breast
> The labouring clouds do often rest.

At first reading, these lines seem hardly worthy of Wordsworth; yet
they conceal, perhaps, a useful indication. The fertile clouds about to
give birth to rain and free themselves of their burden writhe in agony
on the summits of the sterile mountains. "Barren breast" is a figure
not unlike "wanton heed," and "labouring . . . rest" is similar to the
tonal "alert quiet." The calendar of Milton's writing would suggest
that artistic sterility and the struggle for expressive birth were not
far from his mind. The dismissals of the unfruitful melancholy and
the infertile folly join in making firm this presumption. The poems
were, I expect, begotten of a struggle; they partially tell the history
of this struggle; and they outline the process that will lead to the
eventual fecundation of the poet's imagination. But to return to
Tillyard's theses.

There is no doubt that the opening passages of "Il Penseroso" are
less boisterous than those of "L'Allegro," and though the metrical
cursus is similar, Tillyard is tacitly ready to exempt the invocation
of the former poem from censure. The difference between the two
passages is teasing because it may mark a growth of confidence. The
first part of "L'Allegro" obtains much of its loudness from a liberal
use of dental and palatal spirants; the voiceless labial spirant that
controls the second hortation supplies a note of deliberation that is
emphasized by /10/ the delaying quality of the voiced labial stop.
The *mora* in the second invocation is further enhanced by the fact
that the meaning is not immediately clear. It would probably be

somewhat unintelligible to those readers who have no knowledge of
the tropes of Renaissance psychology. What Milton says in the first
poem's invocation is at once obvious: Melancholy born of Midnight
in a dark and horrid place is exiled to a desert cave. In the invocation
to the second poem, he banishes the ungoverned imagination, setting
aside delusions fostered by irrational thought. The mode of the first
invocation is rejection; that of the second, though rejection is there,
perpends the grave theme of the poem.

   The second invocation is more accomplished and so is the poem
that it introduces. In "L'Allegro" there is an abrupt division between
the invitation and the main body of the poem. This is not true of
"Il Penseroso." "To hear the lark" comes as a separate verse paragraph after the variation on the Elizabethan "come-live-with-me-and-
be-my-love" motif. The transition in "Il Penseroso" between the invitation to Contemplation and Silence and the phrase " 'Less Philomel
will deign a song" is more fluid and skillful. The poetic components
of "Il Penseroso" seem to glide out of each other by brilliant acts of
association. Pursuing the moon, the poet, like Endimion, finds himself
climbing towards her on a hillside. From this point he more readily
hears the notes of the curfew as they are carried by the stream of air.
But the air is uncongenial so he retires to his fire and seated before
it hears the snugger voices of the cricket and the bellman. One phrase
naturally follows another; they are not appliqued to the piece as they
are in "L'Allegro."

   I have said that these poems have little social quality, that the
poet lives to himself. It is for this reason that "Il Penseroso" gains
in power; it is much more solitary and, hence, a more personal poem.
Although Milton had previously declaimed against Night in the
prolusion, his experiences of night as he relates them in the second
poem were certainly more keenly felt than the experiences recounted
in "L'Allegro." /11/ Books read are part of this autobiography but only
the most obvious part. "*Cynthia* checks her Dragon yoke, / Gently
o'er th' accustom'd Oak." The oak is real, and when Milton wrote
that passage, he remembered it in all its nocturnal convolutions. The
same may be said of the minutiae of the morning shower:

<blockquote>

usher'd with a shower still,
When the gust hath blown his fill,
Ending on the rustling Leaves,
With minute drops from off the Eaves.

</blockquote>

These lines have in them a conviction of observation that is quite
beyond that of the traditional descriptions of the first poem. A similar
conviction evolves from the particularity of the momentary dream

in the "close covert by some Brook." This is "the bee loud glade," but Milton was there first. The commentators who have tiresomely uncovered analogues for many passages of "L'Allegro" are halted by these figures, for they are not borrowed but are rather the slow distillations of the poet's life.

The differences between these two poems lead me to suppose that "Il Penseroso" is a more mature poem than "L'Allegro," and though I cannot think of either poem as written as an appendix to the prolusion—as the prolusion seems to have been spoken as an appendix to a college play—yet I am ready to suppose that "L'Allegro" is a somewhat younger effort. I want to read these poems together, to hear them as the poet's plans for himself outlined in a series of rising steps; and so it is with reluctance that I think of them, if not poetically separate, as at least temporally apart. "L'Allegro" may have been written during the last years at Cambridge; it may have sprung directly from the prolusion though its purpose was not, I hope, to make the men of Christ's grin. "Il Penseroso" is the poem of a poet who has found his way. It magnifies some of the insights of "L'Allegro," but it is the work of a man who is almost free from the sterile melancholy that once invested him. In the second poem, Milton is not only purged of his black bile but of his academic obligations; he is cultivating his "trim /12/ Gardens" in the "retired leasure" that is proper to his temperament.

To the detriment of the close study of these poems is the trite notion that all that is in them is on the surface, a judgment invariably made on the poetry of young men. Generations, we are told, have taken pleasure in these poems because they have none of the vexing subtilities that obscure Milton's other works. The repetition of this absurdity has disguised the fact that a more sensitive meaning resides in the matter of these poems than has usually been noticed. Yet Milton implies and sometimes openly states that in these poems "more is meant than meets the ear." One of these implications is found in the lines on Chaucer.

> Or call up him that left half told
> The story of *Cambuscan* bold,
> Of *Camball* and of *Algarsife*,
> And who had *Canace* to wife,
> That own'd the virtuous Ring and Glass,
> And of the wond'rous Horse of Brass,
> On which the *Tartar* King did ride.

Here we ask, as we do in the case of Spenser, why this tale of all the *Canterbury Tales* caught the fancy of the poet? There is, of course, something captivating about a fragmentary narrative, but the squire had more than his share of long-windedness and had Chaucer permitted him to finish his story, he might have been telling it yet. I expect that Milton was not so interested in the tale as in the symbolic emphases: the ring, the glass, the brass horse, not the magic sword. The horse conquered space; the mirror made known the secrets of men; and the ring, those of nature. Spenser was charmed with the theme of courtesy and with a court similar to Gloriana's; Milton was enchanted by the symbols of intellectual power. There is a connection that is probably not entirely fortuitous between Chaucer's

> Ther is no foul that fleeth under the hevene
> That she ne shal wel understonde his stevene, /13/
> And knowe his mening openly and pleyn,
> And answere him in his langage ageyn
> And every gras that groweth up-on rote
> She shal eek knowe, and whom it wol do bote   (149-54).

and Milton's

> Where I may sit and rightly spell
> Of every Star that Heav'n doth shew,
> And every Herb that sips the dew.

We do not know how the seventeenth century read Chaucer, but I think that we can assume that Milton saw in this tale a symbolic narrative and that this perception had something to do with the effluence of his two poems.

But this passage does not stand alone in its suggestiveness; another may be fittingly adduced:

> Where I may oft out-watch the *Bear*,
> With thrice great *Hermes*, . . .

The mechanics of Ursa Major have been elucidated by the commentators who inform us that it never sets. Milton, however, out-distances his editors for he directs us to the Ποιμανδρης where we learn that this constellation is a symbol of perfection, of a never declining motion that makes an exact circle around Polaris. "The Bear who revolves upon herself, and carries round with her the whole Kosmos."[3] But how may this concept of perfection be realized? "Thrice great *Hermes*" joins with the "spirit of Plato" to instruct us. The Ποιμανδρης

---

[3]*Op. cit.*, V. 4.

written by the eldest philosopher, as Milton thought of him, flows
into the *Timaeus* written by the best. Plato's achievement of the realm
of essences is well known; Hermes' advice has a Christian condition
that must have entranced the young poet. "The immortal mind that
hath forsook / Her mansion in this fleshly nook," writes Hermes,
proceeds upward and discards some of its material tatters at each of
the spheres. /14/

> And thereupon, having been stripped of all that was wrought
> upon him by the structure of the heavens, he ascends to the
> substance of the eighth sphere, being now possessed of his own
> proper power; and he sings, together with those who dwell there,
> hymning the Father; and they that are there rejoice with him at
> his coming. And being made like to those with whom he dwells,
> he hears the Powers, who are above the substance of the eighth
> sphere, singing praise to God with a voice that is theirs alone.
> And thereafter, each in his turn, they mount upward to the
> Father; they give themselves up to the Powers, and becoming
> Powers themselves, they enter into God.[4]

The mind purified of its mundane excrescences becomes the music
of God. The earthly expression of this experience,

> There let the pealing Organ blow
> To the full voic'd Quire below,
> In Service high and Anthems clear,
> As may with sweetness, through mine ear,
> Dissolve me into extasies,
> And bring all Heav'n before mine eyes,

becomes in its ultimate experience a knowable reality.

This knowable reality is not attained through an excess of religious
emotions or through the exercises of the mystic, but through universal
knowledge as a prelude to universal thought. Hermes displays the
chart of necessary experiences.

> Leap clear of all that is corporeal, and make yourself grow to
> a like expanse with that greatness which is beyond all measure;
> rise above all time, and become eternal; then you will apprehend
> God. Think that for you too nothing is impossible; deem that you
> too are immortal, and that you are able to grasp all things in
> your thought, to know every craft and every science; find your
> home in the haunts of every living creature; make yourself higher

---

[4]*Ibid.,* I. 25-26.

than all heights, and lower than all depths; bring together in
yourself all opposites of quality, heat and cold, dryness and
fluidity; think that you are everywhere at once, on land, at sea,
in heaven; think that you /15/ are not yet begotten, that you are
in the womb, that you are young, that you are old, that you have
died, that you are in the world beyond the grave; grasp in your
thought all this at once, all times and places, all substances and
qualities and magnitudes together; then you can apprehend God.[5]

By this intellectual effort those who have *gnosis* will know God. It is
the culminating point of Hermes' philosophy. Though the end is
different in that it predicts a preparation for an experience rather
than the experience itself, the particularized proposal of the Cambridge student who wrote the third prolusion is similar in intent.

How much better it would be, fellow students, and how much
more worthy of your name, to make at this time a tour as it were
with your eyes about the whole earth as represented on the map
and view the places trodden by ancient heroes, and to travel
through the regions made famous by wars, by triumphs, and even
by the tales of illustrious poets: now to cross the raging Adriatic,
now to approach unharmed flame-capped Aetna; then to observe
the customs of men and the governments of nations, so admirably
arranged; thence to investigate and to observe the natures of all
living creatures; from these to plunge the mind into the secret
powers of stones and plants. Do not hesitate, my hearers, to fly
even up to the skies, there to behold those multiform aspects of
the clouds, the massy power of the snow, and the source of those
tears of early morn; next to peer into the caskets of the hail and
to survey the arsenals of the thunderbolts. Nor let what Jupiter or
Nature veils from you be concealed when a baleful and enormous
comet ofttimes threatens a conflagration from heaven; nor let the
most minute little stars be hidden from you, however many there
may be scattered and straying between the two poles. Yea, follow
as companion the wandering sun, and subject time itself to a
reckoning and demand the order of its everlasting journey. Nay,
let not your mind suffer itself to be hemmed in and bounded by
the same limits as the earth, but let it wander also outside the
boundaries of the world. Finally, what is after all the most important matter, /16/ let it learn thoroughly to know itself and at the
same time those holy minds and intelligences, with whom hereafter it will enter into everlasting companionship.[6]

---

[5] *Ibid.*, XI. 20b.
[6] *Works* (New York, 1936), XII, 169-71.

The talented youth has some of the professional philosopher's abstract boldness and his procedure has a certain likeness to that of the hermetic thinker. This procedure explains the total structure of the two poems.

About the time that Milton was summarizing his method in prose, he made a verse attempt that adumbrates the process of "L'Allegro" and "Il Penseroso"

> Yet I had rather, if I were to choose,
> Thy service in some graver subject use,
> Such as may make thee search thy coffers round,
> Before thou clothe my fancy in fit sound:
> Such where the deep transported mind may soar
> Above the wheeling poles, and at Heav'n's door
> Look in, and see each blissful Deity ·
> How he before the thunderous throne doth lie,
> Listening to what unshorn *Apollo* sings
> To th' touch of golden wires, while *Hebe* brings
> Immortal Nectar to her Kingly Sire:
> Then passing through the Spheres of watchful fire,
> And misty Regions of wide air next under,
> And hills of Snow and lofts of piled Thunder,
> May tell at length how green-ey'd *Neptune* raves,
> In Heav'n's defiance mustering all his waves;
> Then sing of secret things that came to pass
> When Beldam Nature in her cradle was;
> And last of Kings and Queens and *Heroes* old,
> Such as the wise *Demodocus* once told
> In solemn Songs at King *Alcinous'* feast,
> While sad *Ulysses'* soul and all the rest
> Are held with his melodious harmony
> In willing chains and sweet captivity (29-52).

The movement in these lines from "Hail native Language" is downward and the tone is pagan; in the later poems the total /17 /direction is reversed. The structure of "L'Allegro" and "Il Penseroso" is based on a daily but continued ascent. The revolution of the earth presents at each degree of its rotation a new gradation by which the poet rises towards a comprehension of his created end, towards the "everlasting companionship" with "holy minds and intelligences." "L'Allegro" describes the lower level of each degree; "Il Penseroso" the higher. By a continued mounting of the slopes of the intellect from common experience, to intellectual experience, to religious inspiration, the poet trusts to arrive at the supreme poetic gratification.

Till old experience do attain
To something like Prophetic strain.

For this reason, the dynamic symbol of the poem is the tower, soli-
tariness and loneliness in itself, but truly much more than that.
Above the horizon of "L'Allegro" stand "Towers and Battlements"
and "Tow'red Cities" directing our attention to the "high lonely Tow'r"
of "Il Penseroso." This is the most important tower because it has no
existence outside the mind of the poet. It is, in fact, his mind and in
its immateriality it is similar to the "watch-tow'r" that stands above
the early lines of "L'Allegro." Both towers have a supraphysical reality
and for that reason they cast long shadows on the flatter physical
aspects of the poems. There is, of course, a literal interpretation of
the "lonely tower" which the Renaissance would quickly comprehend.
Luther wrote in a tower; Don Quixote read his Palmerin and his
Amadis in a high room over his courtyard; Montaigne, having returned
home to recline on the bosoms of the learned virgins, lived in a tower.
Milton's tower is different; it is at once a refuge and a beacon. It may
be explicated anagogically.

As the midnight lamp shone down on the pages of the *Timaeus*, it
lighted the passage, I imagine, where the mind of man is compared to
a tower, an ἀκρόπολις, from which orders dictated by the reason were
dispatched to the body (70a). The critical gloss on this passage would
have referred the reader to /18/ the *Republic*, where the mind is said
to be the watch-tower of the soul τῆς ψυχῆς ἀκρόπολιν (560b). Other
Greeks seized on this analogy and by transcription it became the *arx* of
the Latins. Pliny uses it so[7] and Cicero proclaims the mind the mirific
tower of the body.[8] It is one of those self-propagating images and, col-
lated with Hebraic usages, it penetrated the writings of the Christian
Church and found a place in English poetry. Spenser knows this tower
and makes it the citadel of Alma's house; Donne urges his readers
to ascend to the "watchtowre."[9] It congregates with the admonition of
Isaiah, "*contemplare in specula*" and with the response: "My lord,
I stand continually upon the watchtower in the daytime, and I am
set in my ward whole nights."[10] The earthly tower is equated with
alertness, with continued intellectual and devotional occupation. The
poet must inhabit the tower so that he can find the cell. Here, attended
by the "Cherub Contemplation" he must examine his "old experience"

----

[7]*Hist. Nat.*, XI. 134.
[8]*De Nat. Deor.*, II. 140.
[9]"The Second Anniversary," 290-300.
[10]XXI. 5, 8.

until he has transformed it into the "prophetic strain." Common experience is the way to the tower; intellectual experience is the tower; total experience is the substance of the poems.

The structure of the poems rests on the rising stairs of the tower. It is the symbol of the poet's program of artistic progress, though for the moment it is only confusedly envisioned. The mature Milton will return to this notion again in his account of the once possible evolution of man towards the angelic state,[11] but at that time he will know that it is a concept incapable of realization, a betraying myth, yet then he will also have acquired the gratification that these poems postulate. But when he wrote these poems the gratification was not yet his, and the agony of their composition comes from the fact that though he could see the end as through a mist, he was not sure of his direction. As he writes, the way becomes brighter and finally he can plot the total distance. /19/

The first milestone in the course is measured by the common experiences recorded in "L'Allegro": the plowman, the milkmaid, the mower, the shepherd, the rustic scene, tourneys of arms and wit, the festival of marriage, the theater, the orchestra. All of these experiences are escorted by secular music that is lacking in polyphony: the song of the lark, the crowing of the cock, the whistling of the plowman, the singing of the milkmaid, the hum of the whetstone on the scythe, the music of the bells and the rebeck, the melic softness of Lydian airs. The eventual union of verse and music is the guidepost to "Il Penseroso" where common experience fades away but the music continues. The uninterrupted flow of harmonious sound between the two poems is personified and differentiated by the sundered emphases on the Orphic legend. In "L'Allegro" Orpheus hears the music; it is given to him from "the hidden soul of harmony." In "Il Penseroso" the embodied soul of Orpheus makes the music that forces "Hell grant what Love did seek." The natural poetry of the first phrasing is passive; it comes without struggle. In the second stage, the poet, called into a new life, reproduces the song in a kind of second creation.

The second milestone is the tower. Common experience is shut out and secular music is subdued because the experience here is of the mind and particular. Alone, separated from the enticements of sensation, the poet finds in the writings of those who have reached the final gratification the necessary invigorating intellectual experience. This is a higher experience than that of "L'Allegro" but the first experience promotes the second; it is the rise of the step but not the

---

[11]*Paradise Lost*, V. 469-503.

tread. The difference and the similarity between the two may be
translated by the dreams of "L'Allegro" and "Il Penseroso." The poet
of "L'Allegro" dreams "on Summer eves by haunted streams" of the
purely secular: pomp, feast, revelry, masks, antique pageantry, the
matter of common experience. The poet of "Il Penseroso" has a
"strange mysterious dream" not easily glossed by the ordinary experience of men. The dream is one of the steps in the progress, but the
substance of the dream, though in both instances it is associated with
watery sounds, is different. That of "L'Allegro" is on a slightly inferior
level to that of /20/ "Il Penseroso," yet it constitutes the rise of the
step. The total process is contained in the last thirty lines of the
second poem, "where more is meant than meets the ear." To make a
closer reading possible, I reprint the lines.

> There in close covert by some Brook,
> Where no profaner eye may look,
> Hide me from Day's garish eye,
> While the Bee with Honied thigh,
> That at her flow'ry work doth sing,
> And the Waters murmuring
> With such consort as they keep,
> Entice the dewy-feather'd Sleep;
> And let some strange mysterious dream
> Wave at his Wings in Airy stream,
> Of lively portraiture display'd,
> Softly on my eye-lids laid.
> And as I wake, sweet music breathe
> Above, about, or underneath,
> Sent by some spirit to mortals good,
> Or th'unseen Genius of the Wood.
> But let my due feet never fail
> To walk the studious Cloister's pale,
> And love the high embowed Roof,
> With antic Pillars massy proof,
> And storied Windows richly dight,
> Casting a dim religious light.
> There let the pealing Organ blow
> To the full voic'd Quire below,
> In Service high and Anthems clear,
> As may with sweetness, through mine ear,
> Dissolve me into extasies,
> And bring all Heav'n before mine eyes.
> And may at last my weary age
> Find out the peaceful hermitage,

> The Hairy Gown and Mossy Cell,
> Where I may sit and rightly spell
> Of every Star that Heav'n doth shew,
> And every Herb that sips the dew;
> Till old experience do attain
> To something like Prophetic strain. /21/

These lines give the immediate effect of a rhapsodic epitome of ascending passion repeated on two sensory tones and proclaiming the ultimate gratification, the end of the poet's progress, now glimpsed but as yet not consummated. There is a ritualistic solemnity about the opening phrases: "Where no profaner eye may look." A mystery is about to take place and the uninitiated are dismissed. This aura of mystery is magnified when we remember that St. Melancholia's face was too bright "to hit the Sense of human sight" and that, as a consequence, it was covered with a dark veil, much as the face of a god is hidden when he shows himself to men. The mystery is further amplified by the two sensory tones of sight and sound, constantly invoked throughout the two poems, and the superior ministers of this whole passage. *Eye* and *ear* are the reiterated words. But there is a difference between the sensations of sight and sound in these closing verses and this difference is made stout by a purple line of demarcation that runs almost through the center of the passage. "But let my due feet never fail" is a frontier; what is north of it is unlike what is south.

The first seventeen lines of this concluding passage lead us back to "L'Allegro." "Such sights as youthful Poets dream / On Summer eves by haunted stream" collates in a way with the morning brook, the murmuring water, and the dream of "Il Penseroso," but the emphasis in counterdistinction is on youth, the beginning of things. Though similar, their dreams are not the same. The dream of "L'Allegro" is slighter in substance, common in poetic experience, and it leads to the sham reality of the theater and the "wanton heed" and "giddy cunning" of Lydian music. The dream of "Il Penseroso" is of a far higher order, a "strange mysterious dream" which is succeeded by a mysterious music, "above, about, or underneath." This music, unlike that which arouses Orpheus from his "golden slumber," cannot be identified or localized. It may be the music of the spheres. It may be the song of Apollo. The poet does not know. It is sent, perhaps, by a spirit to "mortals good"—*good* is, I expect, a master word—or by the genius of the place. The connections with the earlier passages are telling, /22/ but this section of the latter lines leads ineluctably to the conclusion.

The music is once again re-echoed in the music of the church which is neither natural nor inexplainable. The great polyphonic organ is above; the multivoiced quire is below; together they make the full throat of the universe. Verse and voice are married here. The ear is fully charged. The pictures—gifts to sight—are also identified. In the opening lines of this passage, portraits are laid softly on the eyelids of the sleeping poet; in the last lines these portraits become the "storied Windows richly dight" of the church. What was without reality in the earlier expression has shape and substance at the end. The common experience of the poet is transmogrified into a poetic experience that can be grasped by the aesthetic faculties. But the poet gets from the covert to the church through the "studious cloister." The cloister is the synonym for the tower in Milton's lexicon of symbols. The route of the progress is now mapped; common experience refined by intellectual experience makes for the highest sort of poetic experience. We are carefully informed that this is not ordinary poetic experience; the church, in a larger sense, assures an alteration of manner. In the church the theme of sight and sound, of pictures and music, unite in a powerful concluding succession.

> As may with sweetness, *through mine ear,*
> Dissolve me into extasies,
> And bring all Heav'n *before mine eyes.*

The universal music of the church, so unlike Lydian music or the strange tunes heard by the natural poet, effects a dream more profound and miraculous than that of the poet of "L'Allegro" or the "strange mysterious dream" with which the passage begins. "All Heav'n" takes the place of "Shallow Brooks, and Rivers wide." But there is still one more furlong in the journey.

Common experience, intellectual experience, poetic experience are not enough. The "Prophetic strain" is the child of "old experience," which is all of this experienced over and over /23/ again. The direction of the poems is that of a continued venture, and we must think of the poet as writing these poems tomorrow, the day after, and for years to come. As the Bear makes its relentless circle in the skies, the tireless poet must repeat this circle on earth and insatiately observe the ritual of the progress. When the final poem was written, the agony was finished because the way to the ultimate gratification was known, but there must be no slumber, no relapse into "loathed melancholy," only a ceaseless passing from one chamber of experience to the next.

Rosemund Tuve

From The Structural Figures of *L'Allegro* and *Il Penseroso**

For the subject of *L'Allegro* is every man's Mirth, our Mirth, the
very Grace herself with all she can include. Therefore its images are
not individualized. Milton does not describe a life, or a day, but
through images causes us to recall, imagine, and savor the exact
nature of joy when it is entirely *free* of that fetter, which ties down
the joys we actually experience in an order of reality that does not
present us with essences pure. Therefore Eliot will not find here his
'particular milkmaid', for this one must instead be all milkmaids who
ever sang; she must even be whatever fresh singing creature, not a
milkmaid, does bring the same joy to the heart of him to whom
milkmaids bring it not. The Plowman forever whistling, and the
Mower who whets his scythe, do not exist thus simplified and quin-
tessential in Nature, yet the fresh delight these catch for us lives in
every such one we see—see with the eyes, that is, of one admitted of
Mirth's crew. That is precisely the grace she confers. It is the first
secret of this imagery that it does not speak only of what it mentions,
rather provides a channel along which our perhaps barely similar
experiences flow straight and full to a single meaning.

A second secret is that they do this *in despite of* sorrow, like the
lark which is just one of all the creatures of earth who in these
moments seem to take man into a fellowship of ease and /21/ inno-
cence. It is a strength of pastoral imagery, especially that bordering
upon the 'pathetic fallacy', that it conveys 'that mutual exchange
of good will' which has been given as one definition of the late

---

*Reprinted from *Images and Themes in Five Poems by Milton.* Cambridge,
Massachusetts: Harvard University Press, 1957, pp. 15-36. Copyright, 1957, by the
President and Fellows of Harvard College. Reprinted by permission of the publisher
and the executor of the author's estate. Only pp. 20-26, 33-36 are reprinted here.

Renaissance allegorized meaning of 'the Graces'.[1] Milton's landscape
of lawns and fallows, with its nibbling flocks and bare breasts of
mountains, just so sets sorrow at naught. The reasons for it are too
profound to examine here, but that which lies behind an earthly
paradise archetype in terms of mountain-flowers-trees-and-birds, and
that which made men connect freedom, the country, and holidays,
long before they were penned in cities, operates to make us walk with
secure well-being through the world of *L'Allegro's* images.[2] We frame
it meanwhile to the shape of our own minds and experiences.

Various explanations have been given for this immediacy in the
imagery. I do not believe[3] that it results either from simplicity of outline compelling us to fill in our own detail, or from an image-technique
which though it chiefly generalizes is capable also of realistic 'indi-
vidualizing' when the sensibility is awakened (for example, the drip-
ping eaves of *Il Penseroso*). Either these are not the factors which
matter, or some other is unnoted. This can be tested by the generalized
four-line figure of the Sun as king, or the genre-painting image of the
Cock with its accompanying military metaphor, ' . . . with lively din,
Scatters the rear of darkness thin' (two of the very few uses of
metaphor within single images). We are as obedient to participate
in these more elaborate images as in Till- /22/ yard's cited case of the
cottage with its mere 'two aged Okes'. *Golden slumber* on the 'heapt
Elysian flowres' is as 'real' as the *tanned* haycock. What is *real* is the
experience of pleasure we have through each of them. This experience
is sporadically rather than necessarily connected with sensuous precision. Not one of all these is individualized. They are not 'individuals',
unique sights seen by one man's eye, but particulars, irradiated by
the 'general' which they signify: a fresh and vivid joy such as we
take in living itself—or could, were it but care-less.

This seems to me the answer to the much-discussed 'generalness' of
the images of these two poems—a bad word for a great virtue. They
have it because of the nature of the two subjects, and it is in no way

---

[1]See **D. G. Gordon**, 'Ben Jonson's Haddington Masque: the Story and the Fable',
Modern Language Review, XLII (1947), p. 186.

[2]The landscapes and birds and groves of *Il Penseroso* all point a different direction. Mere content (area providing the 'vehicle') determines the nature of no image
save public symbols. Innumerable niceties of language, of rhetorical scheme and
rhythm, of associated story, *require* us to see a different 'general' shining through
Il Penseroso's particulars (examples of these three ways of differentiating so-called
nature images are: 'Heav'ns wide *pathles* way', 70; 'Swinging slow with sullen roar',
76; Philomel, 56-64).

[3]With Tillyard, or with D. C. Allen . . . , both of whom cite the eaves image,
Il Penseroso 129.

at odds with particularity, only with individuality. Perhaps it is
this virtue which makes natural another effect, quite as unexpected
(except in rhetorical theory, which directs us to both) as this convey-
ing of 'reality' without the 'realism' of portraying single objects. We
have a sense that Milton has covered his subject. Turning, our 'eye
hath caught new pleasures'—and lo when we have walked through
two or three meadows with nothing in them except a daisy here and
there, and past the towers in the tufted trees and the cottage, we
seem to have known all that the phrase can mean, 'the pleasures of
the eye'. In the 'Towred Cities' which break the horizon line before
us we approach all those we know or imagine, and hear the 'busie
humm' of every festivity enjoyed in any of them; the feasts and
revels so few and indistinct (to our senses) yet leave no such gaieties
unincluded, just as all the innumerable variations which a lifetime
can put into the phrase 'the pleasures of books' are taken care of by
Il Penseroso's little seventeenth-century list. One supposes that this
sense of completeness is another result of the functioning of images
when their subject is a 'general' or universal, and they are in decorous
relation to it. /23/

The unindividualized character of the images is matched in the
time-structure of the poems. It seems to be taken for granted by most
recent writers on the imagery proper, and is necessary to the main
theses of some of these, that Milton's major concern is to portray the
full round of a day, the 'pensive man's day' beginning with evening,
but both 'days' progressing straightforwardly through time and all
but constituting the poems' subjects. This is surely not quite accurate.
There are various *days* in *L'Allegro*; one of them lasts all through a
Sunshine Holyday, when '*sometimes*' in one of the upland hamlets
there is dancing in the chequer'd shade until the live-long day-light
fails and the tales begin—and we do not know for sure how much
of this revel we join. 'Oft' the speaker listens to the hunt (he does
not see, but thinks of, the way a hill still dew-covered looks *hoar*).
Thereupon we hear of him '*Som time* walking' on the green hillocks
over against where the sun begins his state. Nor can we certainly tell
whether we are to imagine as actually attended the pomps and feasts,
at court, for they not only are set in cities, but culminate in the
dubious appositive, 'Such sights as youthful Poets dream On Summer
eeves by haunted stream'. Surely, as we should expect from 'admit
me . . . to live with thee', we do follow roughly through the most
usual unit into which we divide the passage of time as we live it, but
not nearly closely enough for this to indicate the significance of each
whole poem's images, nor are the first thirty-seven and sixty-two lines,

respectively, thus to be set aside as extraneous to their pattern. Actions take place both in August and June; we watch each: Phillis leaves in haste to bind the sheaves, '*Or if* the earlier season', to lead to the haycock in the meadow. The last image—the miraculous imitation of immortal verses so sung that Orpheus who hears them knows why his own music but half regained Eurydice—has no place nor time: '*And ever* against eating Cares. *Lap me* in soft Lydian /24/ Aires...'. Where are we? and whence, and when, does the music sound? This is not *the joyful man's day*. It is *Joy*. 'And if I give thee honour due, Mirth, admit me of thy crue'.

These pleasures are of course not the 'vain deluding joyes' banished at the commencement of *Il Penseroso*. Each poem begins with a banishing of the travesty of what is praised in the other, a common rhetorical device, not unrelated to the method of dialectic which is one ancestor of the Prolusions (of course) and of the whole long tradition of *débats, conflictus* wedded to eclogue, the pastoral 'choice', and the like small kinds. In each case, what is banished is quite real, not the subject of the other poem seen in a different mood, or moral temper. 'Loathed Melancholy', child of death and night, was (and is) the source of a serious mental condition. Serious but not solemn, both banishing-passages have the wit of contrast (with the companion poem, with the personage praised in the remainder of the exordium) and the wit of bringing out the paradoxical but quite true doubleness of that for which we have but one name.[4] For it is a Goddess, *sage* and *holy*, of *Saintly* visage—*divinest* Melancholy—who is indeed the true subject of all of *Il Penseroso*, without qualification and without apology. Her nature is very exactly delineated in it, without waste or irrelevance; the leisurely economy of the images is a primary factor in making the poem what Johnson called it, a noble effort of the imagination. Nobility is a just term for its pre-eminent character, if we make room therein for the delicacy and spacious amplitude with which a sensitive mind grasps and presents a great conception, avoiding doctrinaire rigor and awake to the hair-thin variousness with which men conceive ideas. *Melancholy* is of /25/ course not the conception we call by that name. She presents to the imaging faculty, that the understanding and heart cannot but lay hold of it and desire it, a great humanistic ideal.

It would be folly and presumption, and certainly eludes my competence, to describe with neat labels a conception which not only this

---

[4]Obviously this disagrees with Tillyard's suggestion of a burlesque tone, and Brooks's of an *ironical* contrast, based on the exaggeration of the images. See note [6] for references that give evidence on the *two* melancholy's familiar to the period, also made clear in J. B. Leishman's valuable study of '*L'Allegro* and *Il Penseroso* in their Relation to Seventeenth-Century Poetry', *Essays and Studies*, 1951.

poem but half a dozen moving expositions illuminate at length with ardor and care. It seems to me preferable to speak of places where those who read this essay may pursue such conceptions, usually places where Milton too had almost certainly taken fire from them. In accordance with what one begins to suspect is a universally applicable rule, an informed and deepened understanding of a poem's whole subject provides, more directly than analysis, a changed response to its images. Although Milton's poem stands to suffer more from the trivializing, than the vital mistaking, of its subject, its power and delicately touched seriousness can be so enriched by readings which go beyond what I can include here, that I shall not attempt to be more than a guidepost, nor present fully the philosophical ideas involved.

Since the publication of Panofsky and Saxl's *Dürers "Melencolia I"* in 1923, and certainly since Panofsky's *Albrecht Dürer* in 1943, it has been conveniently open to us to see much more truly certain meanings Milton's major image indubitably has, though since covered over by time and semantic change. No doubt they have been seen and pointed out in a dozen classrooms, and we have simply not got around to a special study applying new knowledge in a critical analysis of the images of *Il Penseroso*, but at any rate the only printed recognitions of a changed conception are the partial ones I mention below in specific connections. The important relevant points in Panofsky's book[5] are: that he brings to the fore the Renaissance popularity of Aristotle's *Problemata*, xxx, with its treatment of the necessary relation between /26/ melancholy and genius (philosophical, political, poetic); that he shows how Ficino was pre-eminent in revising (not inventing anew) the traditional conception of melancholy, leading the way in a humanistic glorification of the Melancholy Man as the type par excellence of the contemplative, the intellectual genius intent upon understanding hidden wisdom; and that he re-examines the connection (again traditional, but repointed) of these ideas with Saturn, the Saturnian man and the planet's influence. Knowledge of this particular strain of meaning for Melancholy was not esoteric or farfetched, and Milton could scarcely have been ignorant of writers such as Ficino, Vives, Fracastoro, Melanchthon, Bodin, Agrippa.[6] A student of mediaeval literature saw such connections with Milton's

---

[5]See the later study (2nd edition, Princeton, 1945), I, 157-171, and also *Studies in Iconology*, esp. pp. 209ff.

[6]Lawrence Babb in *The Elizabethan Malady* (East Lansing, Mich., 1951) gives needed information and relates it (though briefly, pp. 178-180) to the two poems. This does not take the place of familiarity with some Renaissance treatment of the matter. G. W. Whiting's *Milton's Literary Milieu* (Chapel Hill, 1939), has some additional details, as does Leishman (n. [4] above).

poem before these studies came out, for traditional conceptions have
been modified and re-directed rather than quite changed. It still seems
necessary to read some or one of the Renaissance treatments if one
is to realize the artistic implications (on the level of minutiae in the
images) of Milton's use of a figure like 'divinest Melancholy' daughter
of Saturn; exact phraseology and total impression are important when
the task in hand is to recreate a symbolic figure who has lost her
earlier significancy, and worse still taken on an unfitting one with
numerous distractions in the form of unscrutinized associations. . . .
/33/. For the two conceptions to which he has given a shape /34/
Milton found the names Mirth and Melancholy, inherited names for
inherited figures. Just these shapes we shall find nowhere but in these
poems, and uses of light and the things of day do not symbolically
reveal the form of one conception, shadows and night the other. The
two personages are truly figurative in their action, the sole important
figures of any scope, and each is the 'dominant symbol' of her poem—
not light nor darkness nor towers.[7] They do not themselves act out
their natures, and make no allegory (lack the 'continued' character
of allegorical metaphors). After the habit of goddesses (or planets,
or 'generals'), they *govern*—and their servants display the nature of
that rule and its rewards,[8] themselves constituting a praise of her they
serve. Each is 'in' every action or place, sight or sound, in her poem
(especially in the landscapes; often these have *only* the meaning
of *expressing*—sometimes quite temporarily—the universal which the
goddesses *symbolize*); and Mirth's man gradually personifies the Personification, shadows forth the Grace Euphrosyne, not the other way
around. This is the way metaphor acts; particulars declare signifi-
cances. It is not because we look in these poems at symbols of whose
force we remain quite ignorant without aid, that reading elsewhere
about them makes the poems show as more exquisitely just—although
there is a little of this in the case of Melancholy and the allegorized
meaning of the Graces. It is rather because figurative writing is a

---

[7]The two discussions of symbolism in *L'Allegro* and *Il Penseroso* here referred to
are those of Cleanth Brooks and D. C. Allen. Brooks's observation of recurrences
and his precision in reading are often very revealing, in this influential essay as in
all his criticism. I do not think his chief interpretation can stand up, largely for the
reason given in the paragraphs discussing pattern and symbols, and also because
some recurrences seem to depend on noting words while ignoring clearly intended
major meanings. Some of Milton's towers have symbolic force; so do some uses of
light. Few poems lack such uses of language, and they do not constitute 'a basic
symbolism.'
[8]Leishman calls this 'personification giving place to exemplification', but this view
cuts the tie between the universal and all the particulars in which it inheres.

hundred /35/ times more pleasurable when we recognize every nuance of significance.

Had we been born earlier we should have had one more help to the kind of pleasure some readers take in imagery: its perfect decorum, showing that astonishing artistry in the maker which awakens gratitude, a form of literary criticism. It is a help that the author himself had in creating the decorum.

I refer to the fact that a seventeenth-century reader recognized immediately the rhetorical structure of these two poems. By virtue of that recognition he also apprehended immediately the fitness which is the great aesthetic attribute their images exhibit; it is what has made, as Leishman says, almost every phrase memorable. Each poem is 'a praise', the form of 'demonstrative oration' called *encomium*, taught to every grammar-school boy according to the rules in such a handbook as Aphthonius, the one Milton probably studied. The images flow directly out of this rhetorical structure, with its usual 'places', of exordium, of praise by 'what kind he came of'—what nation, ancestors, parents—praise by his 'acts', his gifts of mind, of countenance or quality, friends, actions.[9] It would not surprise one who had written dozens of these praises of this or that 'general', or virtue, or personage, to find certain parallels between Milton's two poems; I too would willingly miss this surprise for the informed amazement of recognizing the imaginativeness and disciplined command with which imagery builds the known but natural form. This structure had a powerful influence upon the lyric, with its related aim of celebrating and praising. The reader /36/ who knew the structure (that is, every educated reader of its time) would not turn the great subject of *Il Penseroso* into 'the pensive man's day', would take in the unity of each poem and something of its relation to the other with a single flash of recognition, and would understand and enjoy the very virtue of the images which has been so much rubbed and questioned—for long tracts of each poem consist of the rhetorical 'circumstances' which can justly and delicately limn out the unseizable through the seizable. Where it is suitable, this can produce images of peculiar power to catch the form of what men live for in the fleeting shapes of how they live; it is necessary to be critically alert

---

[9] I use here F. Johnson's reprint of Rainolde's *Foundation of Rhetoric, 1563* (New York, 1945; see f. 40). But see ch. 8 of *John Milton at St. Paul's School* (New York, 1948) by D. I. Clark; he of course notes the relation I make. There is some treatment of the connections of these matters with the character of 'amplifying' images especially, and with Renaissance lyric theory, in the present writer's *Elizabethan and Metaphysical Imagery* (Chicago, 1947), section 1 of ch. v.

to the suitability. There are good literary reasons for the omission of minor metaphors from these poems.

Our sense that certain works will permanently charm is almost always connected with some structural excellence. The shapely perfection of *L'Allegro* and *Il Penseroso* depends most upon a central figurative conception at the heart of each, and these large formative images have been clarified to us as modern scholarship has cleared away obstructions present since the early 1700's. I have not meant by this emphasis upon modern researches and upon the importance of genre and structure to set aside the work from Warton onward which has annotated the images with sources and parallels. Any student of imagery who despises these cuts himself off from his main necessity: the understanding of the words of the text, made precise only thus through innumerable experiences with contexts. This understanding is not always easy, given a lapse of some hundreds of years and considering certain other differences which separate a Milton from any one of us who look at him. I have ignored some criticism, chiefly modern, of the images of *L'Allegro* and *Il Penseroso*, which seemed rather dedicated to the critical principle that madness in great ones must not unwatched go. No willing student of these poems has been able to resist them.

Suggestions for Papers

People have different views on the date of composition of "L'Allegro" and "Il Penseroso" (e.g., W. R. Parker, E. M. W. Tillyard). From your knowledge of Milton's life and poetry, where would you place the poems?

Discuss similar themes in "L'Allegro" and "Il Penseroso" and other early poems of Milton (e.g., "Elegy I," "Lycidas," and *Comus*). What differences do you see?

Discuss "L'Allegro" and "Il Penseroso" as anticipating themes and stylistic devices later developed by Milton in *Paradise Lost, Paradise Regained,* and *Samson Agonistes.*

Do you believe that "Il Penseroso" is more representative of Milton than "L'Allegro"? Does Milton's biography help you to appreciate the meaning of the poems?

Compare the *First Prolusion* to "L'Allegro" and "Il Penseroso." Do you agree with E. M. W. Tillyard's conclusion that the poems were written for an academic audience and are in the tradition of a rhetorical debate? See George L. Geckle's article for further information.

S. Ernest Sprott, Ants Oras, and Michael Moloney discuss the metrical aspects of "L'Allegro" and "Il Penseroso." How does meter contribute to the tone of each poem? Compare the use of meter and rhyme (octosyllabic couplets) to the form used in "The Nativity Ode" and/or "Death of a Fair Infant Dying of a Cough."

Compare "L'Allegro" and "Il Penseroso" and their eighteenth-century imitations: William Collins, "Pity" and "The Passions"; Thomas Gray, "Hymn to Adversity" and "Ode for Music"; and Thomas Warton, "Pleasures of Melancholy" and "Ode on the Approach of Summer."

How does Milton use parallels and contrasts to develop his two poems?

Are "L'Allegro" and "Il Penseroso" balanced so as to develop tension, or do they build to a climax at the close of "Il Penseroso"?

Discuss the use of religious imagery in "Il Penseroso."

Discuss the use of musical imagery in "L'Allegro" and "Il Penseroso." Can you draw connections between its use in the companion poems and in other poems (e.g., "Nativity Ode," "At a Solemn Music," "Arcades," and *Comus*) by Milton?

Is T. S. Eliot's criticism of the poems valid? If possible, extend your discussion to the handling of visual imagery in *Paradise Lost*.

Critics have described the two poems as a development of a twenty-four hour day. Do you agree?

Critics have discussed the poems as a reflection of the Cavalier and Puritan ways of life, which were prominent in seventeenth-century England. Do you agree?

The following are parodies of "L'Allegro" and "Il Penseroso": George Colman and Robert Lloyd, "To Obscurity" and "To Oblivion" (1759); Anonymous, "Garrulous Man, a Parody upon L'Allegro of Milton" (1777). Discuss the effectiveness of the parodies.

Examine Virgil's *Eclogues* II and VIII and Spenser's *The Shepherd's Calendar* (May, October, December) and discuss the characteristics these pastorals have in common with Milton's companion poems.

Examine the following character sketches by Joseph Hall from *Characters of Virtues and Vices* (1608): the Happy Man, the Humble Man, and the Wise Man. Are they and "L'Allegro" and "Il Penseroso" in the same literary tradition?

Examine the following companion poems and compare their characteristics with those evident in "L'Allegro" and "Il Penseroso": Christopher Marlowe, "The Passionate Shepherd to his Love" and Sir Walter Ralegh, "The Nymph's Reply to the Shepherd"; John Fletcher, "Hence, All You Vain Delights" and William Strode, "Return My Joys."

Discuss "L'Allegro and "Il Penseroso" as early examples of the retirement theme, which flourished in seventeenth and eighteenth-century poetry (e.g., Robert Herrick, "The Hock-Cart"; Andrew Marvell, "Upon Appleton House" and "The Garden"; Ben Jonson, "To Penshurst"; John Denham, *Cooper's Hill*.)

Examine the seventeenth-century commentary on melancholy (Lawrence Babb and J. B. Leishman). How does this help explain the nature of melancholy in "Il Penseroso"?

Evaluate Samuel Johnson's comment: "No mirth can, indeed, be found in his melancholy; but I am afraid that I always meet some melancholy in his mirth."

Evaluate Cleanth Brooks's argument for light symbolism in the twin poems and J. Milton French's criticism of Brooks.

Write a critique on two contrasting essays on "L'Allegro" and "Il Penseroso" (i.e., the strengths and weaknesses of each argument).

What is Milton's attitude toward nature in "L'Allegro" and "Il Penseroso"?

Discuss Milton's handling of classical and Christian materials in "L'Allegro" and "Il Penseroso."

To what extent may the companion poems be said to describe a mystical progression toward communion with God? See Evelyn Underhill's *Mysticism: A Study in the Nature and Development of Man's Spiritual Consciousness* (New York: E. P. Dutton, 1930) for the basic characteristics of mysticism.

Additional Readings

Editions

Brooks, Cleanth and John E. Hardy, editors. *Poems of Mr. John Milton: The 1645 Edition with Essays in Analysis*. New York: Harcourt, Brace and Company, 1951.

Bush, Douglas, editor. *The Complete Poetical Works of John Milton*. Boston: Houghton Mifflin Company, 1965.

Darbishire, Helen, editor. *The Poetical Works of John Milton*. London: Oxford University Press, 1958.

Fletcher, Harris F., editor. *John Milton's Complete Poetical Works Reproduced in Photographic Facsimile*. 4 volumes. Urbana, Illinois: University of Illinois Press, 1943.

Hanford, James H., editor. *The Poems of John Milton*. 2nd edition. New York: Ronald Press Company, 1953.

Hughes, Merritt Y., editor. *John Milton: Complete Poems and Major Prose*. New York: Odyssey Press, 1957.

Masson, David, editor. *The Poetical Works of John Milton*. 3 volumes. 2nd edition. London: Macmillan Company, 1890.

Patterson, Frank A., editor. *The Works of John Milton*. 18 volumes. New York: Columbia University Press, 1931-38.

Prince, F. T., editor. *Milton: Comus and Other Poems*. London: *Milton*. New York: New York University Press, 1963.

Shawcross, John T., editor. *The Complete English Poetry of John Milton*. New York: New York University Press, 1963.

Todd, Henry J., editor. *The Poetical Works of John Milton*. 7 volumes. 2nd edition. London: J. Johnson Publishing Company, 1809.

Verity, Arthur W., editor. *Milton's Ode on the Morning of Christ's Nativity, L'Allegro, Il Penseroso, and Lycidas*. London: Cambridge University Press, 1891.

Reference, Bibliography

Fletcher, Harris F. *Contributions to a Milton Bibliography, 1800-1930.* Urbana, Illinois: University of Illinois Press, 1931.

Huckabay, Calvin. *John Milton: A Bibliographical Supplement, 1929-1957.* Pittsburgh: Duquesne University Press, 1960.

Stevens, David H. *A Reference Guide to Milton from 1800 to the Present Day.* Chicago: University of Chicago Press, 1930.

Milton: Biography

Darbishire, Helen, editor. *The Early Lives of Milton.* London: Constable and Company, Ltd., 1932.

Diekhoff, John S., editor. *Milton on Himself.* New York: Oxford University Press, 1939.

Hanford, James H. *John Milton: Englishman.* New York: Crown Publishers, 1949.

Masson, David. *The Life of John Milton.* 6 volumes. London: Macmillan and Company, 1859-94.

Parker, William R. *Milton: A Biography.* 2 volumes. New York: Oxford University Press, 1968.

L'Allegro and Il Penseroso

Babb, Lawrence. *The Elizabethan Malady.* East Lansing, Mich.: Michigan State College Press, 1951.

Bowling, William Glasgow. "The Travelogue Sections of *L'Allegro* and *Il Penseroso*," *English Journal*, XXV (March, 1936), 220-23.

Brodribb, C. W. "Milton's *L'Allegro* and *Il Penseroso*," *Notes and Queries*, CLXIII (September, 1932), 201.

Carpenter, Nan Cooke. "Spenser's *Epithalamion* as Inspiration for Milton's *L'Allegro* and *Il Penseroso*," *Notes and Queries*, CCI (July, 1956), 289-92.

———. "The Place of Music in *L'Allegro* and *Il Penseroso*," *University of Toronto Quarterly*, XXII (July, 1935), 354-67.

Dorian, Donald C. "The Question of Autobiographical Significance in *L'Allegro* and *Il Penseroso*," *Modern Philology*, XXXI (November, 1933), 175-82.

136 *Additional Readings*

Emerson, Francis W. "Why Milton Uses 'Cambuscan' and 'Camball,' " *Modern Language Notes*, XLVII (March, 1932), 153-54.

Fink, Z. S. "*Il Penseroso*, Line 16," *Philological Quarterly*, XIX (July, 1940), 309-13.

Geckle, George L. "Miltonic Idealism: *L'Allegro* and *Il Penseroso*," *Texas Studies in Language and Literature*, IX (1968), 455-73.

Grace, William J. "Notes on Robert Burton and John Milton," *Studies in Philology*, LII (October, 1955), 578-91.

Halpert, V. B. "On Coming to the Window in *L'Allegro*," *Anglia*, LXXXI (1963), 198-200.

Hanford, James H. "The Youth of Milton: An Interpretation of His Early Literary Development," in *Studies in Shakespeare, Milton, and Donne*, University of Michigan Publications: Language and Literature, I (1925), 89-163.

Havens, Raymond Dexter. *The Influence of Milton on English Poetry*. New York: Russell and Russell, 1961.

Hoeltje, Hubert H. "*L'Allegro*, Lines 53-55," *Publications of the Modern Language Association*, XLV (March, 1930), 201-3.

Howard, H. Wendell. "Milton's *L'Allegro*, 136-143," *Explicator*, XXIV (September, 1965), item 3.

Leavis, F. R. *The Common Pursuit*. London: Chatto and Windus, 1962.

Lowes, John Livingston. "*L'Allegro* and *The Passionate Shepheard*," *Modern Language Review*, XI (April, 1911), 206-9.

Lumiansky, R. M. "Milton's English Again," *Modern Language Notes*, LV (December, 1940), 591-94.

Moloney, Michael F. "The Prosody of Milton's *Epitaph, L'Allegro*, and *Il Penseroso*," *Modern Language Notes*, LXXII (March, 1957), 174-78.

Oras, Ants. "Metre and Chronology in Milton's *Epitaph on the Marchioness of Winchester, L'Allegro and Il Penseroso*," *Notes and Queries*, CXCVIII (August, 1953), 332-33.

Panofsky, Erwin. *Studies in Iconology: Humanistic Themes in the Art of the Renaissance*. New York: Oxford University Press, 1939.

Parker, W. R. "Some Problems in the Chronology of Milton's Early Poems," *Review of English Studies*, XI (July, 1935), 276-83.

Post, Martin M. "Milton's Twin Lyrics at Three Hundred," *English Journal*, XXII (September, 1933), 567-80.

Riggs, Edith. "Milton's *L'Allegro*, 41-50," *Explicator*, XXIII (February, 1965), item 44.

Sprott, S. Ernest. *Milton's Art of Prosody*. Oxford: Basil Blackwell, 1953.

Via, John A. "The Rhythm of Regenerate Experience: *L'Allegro* and *Il Penseroso*" (soon to be published in *Renaissance Papers*).

Watson, Sara Ruth. "Milton's Ideal Day: Its Development as a Pastoral Theme," *Publications of the Modern Language Association*, LVII (June, 1942), 404-20.

Woodhouse, A. S. P. "Notes on Milton's Early Development," *University of Toronto Quarterly*, XIII (October, 1943), 66-101.

General Instructions
For A Research Paper

If your instructor gives you any specific directions about the format of your research paper that differ from the directions given here, you are, of course, to follow his directions. Otherwise, you can observe these directions with the confidence that they represent fairly standard conventions.

A research paper represents a student's synthesis of his reading in a number of primary and secondary works, with an indication, in footnotes, of the source of quotations used in the paper or of facts cited in paraphrased material. A *primary* source is the text of a work as it issued from the pen of the author or some document contemporary with the work. The following, for instance, would be considered primary sources: a manuscript copy of the work; first editions of the work and any subsequent editions authorized by the writer; a modern scholarly edition of the text; an author's comment about his work in letters, memoirs, diaries, journals, or periodicals; published comments on the work by the author's contemporaries. A *secondary* source would be any interpretation, explication, or evaluation of the work printed, usually several years after the author's death, in critical articles and books, in literary histories, and in biographies of the author. In this casebook, the text of the work, any variant versions of it, any commentary on the work by the author himself or his contemporaries may be considered as primary sources; the editor's Introduction, the articles from journals, and the excerpts from books are to be considered secondary sources. The paper that you eventually write will become a secondary source.

Plagiarism

The cardinal sin in the academic community is plagiarism. The rankest form of plagiarism is the verbatim reproduction of someone else's words without any indication that the passage is a quotation. A lesser but still serious form of plagiarism is to report, in your own words, the fruits of someone else's research without acknowledging the source of your information or interpretation.

You can take this as an inflexible rule: every verbatim quotation in your paper must be either enclosed in quotation marks or single-spaced and inset from the left-hand margin and must be followed by a footnote number. Students who merely change a few words or phrases in a quotation and present the passage as their own work are still guilty of plagiarism. Passages of genuine paraphrase must be footnoted too if the information or idea or interpretation contained in the paraphrase cannot be presumed to be known by ordinary educated people or at least by readers who would be interested in the subject you are writing about.

The penalties for plagiarism are usually very severe. Don't run the risk of a failing grade on the paper or even of a failing grade in the course.

Lead-Ins

Provide a lead-in for all quotations. Failure to do so results in a serious breakdown in coherence. The lead-in should at least name the person who is being quoted. The ideal lead-in, however, is one that not only names the person but indicates the pertinence of the quotation.

Examples:

(typical lead-in for a single-spaced, inset quotation)

Irving Babbitt makes this observation about Flaubert's attitude toward women:

(typical lead-in for quotation worked into the frame of one's sentence)

Thus the poet sets out to show how the present age, as George Anderson puts it, "negates the values of the earlier revolution."[7]

Full Names

The first time you mention anyone in a paper give the full name of the person. Subsequently you may refer to him by his last name.

Examples: First allusion—Ronald S. Crane
Subsequent allusions—Professor Crane, as Crane says.

Ellipses

Lacunae in a direct quotation are indicated with *three spaced periods,* in addition to whatever punctuation mark was in the text at the point where you truncated the quotation. *Hit the space-bar of your typewriter between each period.* Usually there is no need to put the ellipsis-periods at the beginning or the end of a quotation.

Example: "The poets were not striving to communi-
          cate with their audience; . . . By and
          large, the Romantics were seeking . . .
          to express their unique personalities."[8]

Brackets

Brackets are used to enclose any material interpolated into a direct quotation. The abbreviation *sic,* enclosed in brackets, indicates that the error of spelling, grammar, or fact in a direct quotation has been copied as it was in the source being quoted. If your typewriter does not have special keys for brackets, draw the brackets neatly with a pen.

Examples: "He [Theodore Baum] maintained that Con-
           fucianism [the primary element in Chinese
           philosophy] aimed at teaching each indi-
           vidual to accept his lot in life."[12]
           "Paul Revear [sic] made his historic ride
           on April 18, 1875 [sic]."[15]

Summary Footnote

A footnote number at the end of a sentence which is not enclosed in quotation marks indicates that only *that* sentence is being documented in the footnote. If you want to indicate that the footnote documents more than one sentence, put a footnote number at the end of the *first* sentence of the paraphrased passage and use some formula like this in the footnote:

[16] For the information presented in this and the
following paragraph, I am indebted to Marvin
Magalaner, Time of Apprenticeship: the Fiction of
Young James Joyce (London, 1959), pp. 81-93.

Citing the Edition

The edition of the author's work being used in a paper should always be cited in the first footnote that documents a quotation from that work. You can obviate the need for subsequent footnotes to that edition by using some formula like this:

⁴ Nathaniel Hawthorne, "Young Goodman Brown," as printed in <u>Young Goodman Brown</u>, ed. Thomas E. Connolly, Charles E. Merrill Literary Casebooks (Columbus, Ohio, 1968), pp. 3-15. This edition will be used throughout the paper, and hereafter all quotations from this book will be documented with a page-number in parentheses at the end of the quotation.

Notetaking

Although all the material you use in your paper may be contained in this casebook, you will find it easier to organize your paper if you work from notes written on 3 x 5 or 4 x 6 cards. Besides, you should get practice in the kind of notetaking you will have to do for other term-papers, when you will have to work from books and articles in, or on loan from, the library.

An ideal note is a self-contained note—one which has all the information you would need if you used anything from that note in your paper. A note will be self-contained if it carries the following information:

(1) The information or quotation *accurately* copied.

(2) Some system for distinguishing direct quotation from paraphrase.

(3) All the bibliographical information necessary for documenting that note—full name of the author, title, volume number (if any), place of publication, publisher, publication date, page numbers.

(4) If a question covered more than one page in the source, the note-card should indicate which part of the quotation occurred on one page and which part occurred on the next page. The easiest way to do this is to put the next page number in parentheses after the last word on one page and before the first word on the next page.

In short, your note should be so complete that you would never have to go back to the original source to gather any piece of information about that note.

Footnote Forms

The footnote forms used here follow the conventions set forth in the *MLA Style Sheet,* Revised Edition, ed. William Riley Parker, which is now used by more than 100 journals and more than thirty university presses in the United States. Copies of this pamphlet can be purchased for fifty cents from your university bookstore or from the Modern Language Association, 62 Fifth Avenue, New York, N.Y. 10011. If your teacher or your institution prescribes a modified form of this footnoting system, you should, of course, follow that system.

A primary footnote, the form used the first time a source is cited, supplies four pieces of information: (1) author's name, (2) title of the source, (3) publication information, (4) specific location in the source of the information or quotation. A secondary footnote is the shorthand form of documentation after the source has been cited in full the first time.

Your instructor may permit you to put all your footnotes on separate pages at the end of your paper. But he may want to give you practice in putting footnotes at the bottom of the page. Whether the footnotes are put at the end of the paper or at the bottom of the page, they should observe this format of spacing: (1) the first line of each footnote should be indented, usually the same number of spaces as your paragraph indentations; (2) all subsequent lines of the footnote should start at the lefthand margin; (3) there should be single-spacing within each footnote and double-spacing between each footnote.

Example:

[10] Ruth Wallerstein, *Richard Crashaw: A Study in Style and Poetic Development,* University of Wisconsin Studies in Language and Literature, No. 37 (Madison, 1935), p. 52.

Primary Footnotes

(The form to be used the *first* time a work is cited)

[1] Paull F. Baum, *Ten Studies in the Poetry of Matthew Arnold* (Durham, N.C., 1958), p. 37.

(book by a single author; p. is the abbreviation of *page*)

[2] René Wellek and Austin Warren, *Theory of Literature* (New York, 1949), pp. 106–7.

(book by two authors; pp. is the abbreviation of *pages*)

[3] William Hickling Prescott, <u>History</u> <u>of</u> <u>the</u> <u>Reign</u> <u>of</u> <u>Philip</u> <u>the</u> <u>Second,</u> <u>King</u> <u>of</u> <u>Spain,</u> ed. John Foster Kirk (Philadelphia, 1871), II, 47.

(an edited work of more than one volume; *ed.* is the abbreviation for "edited by"; note that whenever a volume number is cited, the abbreviation p. or pp. is *not* used in front of the page number)

[4] John Pick, ed., <u>The</u> <u>Windhover</u> (Columbus, Ohio 1968), p. 4.

(form for quotation from an editor's Introduction—as, for instance, in this casebook series; here *ed.* is the abbreviation for "editor")

[5] A.S.P. Woodhouse, "Nature and Grace in <u>The</u> <u>Faerie</u> <u>Queen,</u>" in <u>Elizabethan</u> <u>Poetry</u>: <u>Modern</u> <u>Essays</u> <u>in</u> <u>Criticism</u>, ed. Paul J. Alpers (New York, 1967), pp. 346-7.

(chapter or article from an edited collection)

[6] Morton D. Paley, "Tyger of Wrath," <u>PMLA</u>, LXXXI (December, 1966), 544.

(an article from a periodical; note that because the volume number is cited no p. or pp. precedes the page number; the titles of periodicals are often abbreviated in footnotes but are spelled out in the Bibliography; here, for instance, *PMLA* is the abbreviation for *Publications of the Modern Language Association*)

Secondary Footnotes

(Abbreviated footnote forms to be used after a work has been cited once in full)

[7] Baum, p. 45.

(abbreviated form for work cited in footnote #1; note that the secondary footnote is indented the same number of spaces as the first line of primary footnotes)

[8] Wellek and Warren, pp. 239-40.

(abbreviated form for work cited in footnote #2)

[9] Prescott, II, 239.

(abbreviated form for work cited in footnote #3; because this is a multi-volume work, the volume number must be given in addition to the page number)

[10] <u>Ibid</u>., p. 245.

(refers to the immediately preceding footnote—that is, to page 245 in the second volume of Prescott's history; *ibid.* is the abbreviation of the Latin adverb *ibidem* meaning "in the same place"; note that this abbreviation is italicized or underlined and that it is followed by a period, because it is an abbreviation)

[11] Ibid., III, 103.
(refers to the immediately preceding footnote—that is, to Prescott's work again; there must be added to *ibid.* only what changes from the preceding footnote; here the volume and page changed; note that there is no p. before 103, because a volume number was cited)

[12] Baum, pp. 47-50.
(refers to the same work cited in footnote #7 and ultimately to the work cited in full in footnote #1)

[13] Paley, p. 547.
 (refers to the article cited in footnote #6)

[14] Rebecca P. Parkin, "Mythopoeic Activity in the Rape of the Lock," ELH, XXI (March, 1954), 32.
(since this article from the *Journal of English Literary History* has not been previously cited in full, it must be given in full here)

[15] Ibid., pp. 33-4.
(refers to Parkin's article in the immediately preceding footnote)

Bibliography Forms

Note carefully the differences in bibliography forms from footnote forms: (1) the last name of the author is given first, since bibliography items are arranged alphabetically according to the surname of the author (in the case of two or more authors of a work, only the name of the first author is reversed) ; (2) the first line of each bibliography item starts at the lefthand margin; subsequent lines are indented; (3) periods are used instead of commas, and parentheses do not enclose publication information; (4) the publisher is given in addition to the place of publication; (5) the first and last pages of articles and chapters are given; (6) most of the abbreviations used in footnotes are avoided in the Bibliography.

The items are arranged here alphabetically as they would appear in the Bibliography of your paper.

Baum, Paull F. Ten Studies in the Poetry of Matthew Arnold. Durham, N.C.: University of North Carolina Press, 1958.

Paley, Morton D. "Tyger of Wrath," <u>Publications</u> <u>of</u>
<u>the</u> <u>Modern</u> <u>Language</u> Association, LXXXI (Decem-
ber, 1966), 540-51.

Parkin, Rebecca P. "Mythopoeic Activity in the <u>Rape</u>
<u>of</u> <u>the</u> <u>Lock</u>," <u>Journal</u> <u>of</u> <u>English</u> <u>Literary</u>
<u>History</u>, XXI (March, 1954), 30-8.

Pick, John, editor. <u>The</u> <u>Windhover</u>. Columbus, Ohio:
Charles E. Merrill Publishing Company, 1968.

Prescott, William Hickling. <u>History</u> <u>of</u> <u>the</u> <u>Reign</u> <u>of</u>
<u>Philip</u> <u>the</u> <u>Second</u>, <u>King</u> <u>of</u> <u>Spain</u>. Edited by
John Foster Kirk. 3 volumes. Philadelphia: J.B.
Lippincott and Company, 1871.

Wellek, René and Austin Warren. <u>Theory</u> <u>of</u> <u>Litera-</u>
<u>ture</u>. New York: Harcourt, Brace & World, Inc.,
1949.

Woodhouse, A.S.P. "Nature and Grace in <u>The</u> <u>Faerie</u>
<u>Queene</u>," in <u>Elizabethan</u> <u>Poetry</u>: <u>Modern</u> <u>Essays</u> <u>in</u>
<u>Criticism</u>. Edited by Paul J. Alpers. New York:
Oxford University Press, 1967, pp. 345-79.

*If the form for some work that you are using in your paper is not given
in these samples of footnote and bibliography entries, ask your instructor for advice as to the proper form.*